CYCLING

AN INTRODUCTION TO THE SPORT

Tony Roberts

CYCLING

AN INTRODUCTION TO THE SPORT

Tony Roberts

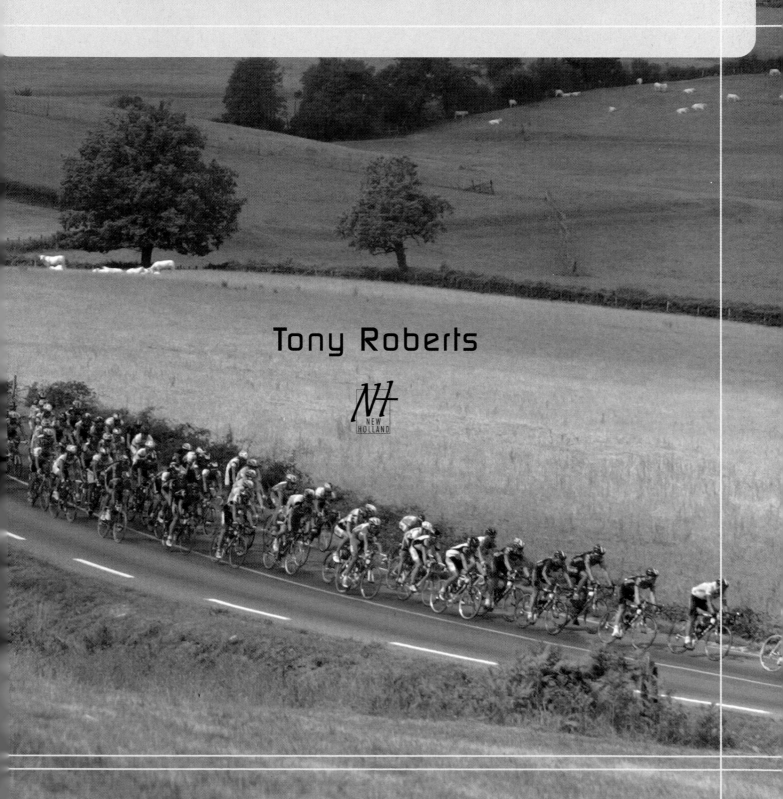

NEW
HOLLAND

First published in 2004 by New Holland Publishers
London • Cape Town • Sydney • Auckland
www.newhollandpublishers.com

86 Edgware Road, London, W2 2EA, United Kingdom
80 McKenzie Street, Cape Town, 8001, South Africa
14 Aquatic Drive, Frenchs Forest, NSW 2086, Australia
218 Lake Road, Northcote, Auckland, New Zealand

Publishing managers	Claudia dos Santos & Simon Pooley
Commissioning editor	Alfred LeMaitre
Publisher	Mariëlle Renssen
Studio manager	Richard MacArthur
Concept design	Samantha Bainbridge
Designer	Gillian Black
Design assistant	Jeannette Streicher
Editor	Anna Tanneberger
Illustrator	Helen Dittmar
Picture researcher	Karla Kik
Proofreader/Indexer	Michelle Coburn
Production	Myrna Collins
Editorial consultants	Company of Cyclists (UK)
	Candice Ridge, Bike.com (USA)

Reproduction by Unifoto, Cape Town
Printed and bound in Malaysia by Times Offset (M) Sdn. Bhd.
10 9 8 7 6 5 4 3 2 1

CONTENTS

ABOVE *A vélocipède race in Bordeaux, 1868.*
LEFT *The starting line.*

BACKGROUND TO CYCLING

This book is an introduction to the sport of cycling. The cyclist we have in mind is rather more enthusiastic than the individual who just uses the bicycle as a vehicle for transport.

The sport has become organized worldwide, enabling cyclists to ride events in many parts of the world. These include the 'centuries' popular in North America, the Randonneur and cyclo-sportif events in Western Europe; and international mass-participation events. The world circuit of the Golden Bike series attracts huge numbers of what the French dub *cyclo-touristes*.

Cycling provides many benefits over and above the activity itself, and beyond the rider's original reason for starting.

Riding, at whatever level of intensity, is an easy introduction to a pattern of regular exercise, which has wide-ranging benefits. Cycling is a low-impact activity, which is less harmful to the joints and can be practised at any age. Studies have demonstrated the benefits to society of a healthy population in terms of increased productivity, fewer man-hours lost due to ill health, lower health costs, and better quality of life. It is an enjoyable way to get regular exercise, fresh air and an improvement in fitness, to escape the urban environment into the solitude of a local country road – a gentle ride alone on narrow, seldom-travelled byways. The experience of travelling to places under your own power and becoming a part of the surroundings is a reward in itself. It can be a low-cost means of touring foreign places, or an add-on to a camping holiday.

The sport enables the cyclist to enjoy camaraderie and companionship or to give vent to his competitive spirit in races.

There are other, less obvious, benefits to cycling – for instance, as a form of urban commuting it helps society by reducing air and noise pollution.

Regardless of what first drew you to the sport, the bicycle's greatest benefit is the freedom it bestows on the rider. It is a freedom that can only really be understood by those who ride the open road.

MICHAUX VELOCIPEDE

A LITTLE BIT OF HISTORY

THE ORIGIN OF THE MACHINE

No-one invented the bicycle. Not the machine we know and recognize as a bicycle today. It evolved.

Before the end of the 18th century, the only vehicles powered by human muscle power were primitive three- or four-wheeled carriages reflecting an idea that had not yet found its time.

In 1817 Karl, Baron Drais von Sauerbronn patented a design for a wooden-framed, steerable machine with two wheels. This resulted in a practical vehicle with which it was possible to cover long distances with greater ease and in less time than a walking man. The bike was still powered by feet on the ground. This was the draisine, named after its inventor.

The success of this machine spread to neighbouring countries and across the Channel to England. By 1820 the first one had reached New York.

Soon inventors in many countries were seeking alternative methods of propulsion in an effort to improve the draisine. A Scottish blacksmith, named Kirkpatrick Macmillan, is credited with being the first to produce a pedal-operated, two-wheeled vehicle. It was rear-wheel propelled via a treadle transmission. A commemorative plaque adorns the forge where, in 1839, he is said to have produced his bicycle. It calls him 'the inventor of the bicycle'. However, without its predecessors like the the draisine, Macmillan might have done nothing more than shoe horses – and our modern cyclist might have ridden a very different vehicle.

TOP The draisine, invented by Baron von Drais.

LEFT Early riders scooted the bike along with their feet on the ground.

ABOVE Kirkpatrick Macmillan fitted treadles to propel the rear wheel.

PLAYER'S CIGARETTES

"ROVER" SAFETY BICYCLE

DEVELOPMENT THROUGH RACING

For 20 years after Macmillan's effort there was no serious attempt to improve the machine. Then a small Parisian manufacturer, Pierre Michaux, built a draisine with a cranked arm and pedals to drive the front wheel. This was quickly developed into a usable vehicle and named the vélocipède. In England it was known as the boneshaker.

By 1865 the Michaux company was producing 400 vélocipèdes a year. The first race was held at St Cloud, Paris, on 31 May 1868. It was won by Englishman James Moore. The next year, more than 200 riders started the Paris-Rouen race. James Moore won again, covering the 123km (76 miles) in less than 10½ hours.

Cycling had arrived. Cycle tracks were established in

major centres, the first cycling publications appeared and the first bicycle show was held.

The early cycling champions quickly became household names. Racing accelerated the technical development of the machine as riders sought mechanical advantages over their rivals – both the champions and those for whom cycling had become a pastime as well as a competitive sport. The increasing demand for the Michaux bicycles could not be met by the factory and alternative manufacturers sprang up, not only in France but also in neighbouring countries.

Mass-production of bicycles began when the Paris agent of the English-based Coventry Sewing Machine Company, Rowley Turner, took a Michaux back to the factory in England. He convinced management to supplement the flagging sewing machine trade and use their production facilities and skills to produce bicycles. This started a period of bicycle production that saw

Coventry become the world capital of bicycle manufacture.

The racing bicycle continued to develop from the Michaux pattern, with the front wheel driven by cranks and pedals. However, with pedals and cranks attached directly to the front wheel, the speed of a Michaux was a function of wheel size. The size of the front wheel gradually increased for greater speed, until it reached limits imposed by the physical length of the rider's leg. This was known as the high-wheeler, or penny-farthing.

The development of the roller chain brought about a change in direction, and led to the development of the Rover Safety Bicycle in England, which looked more like the bicycle as we know it today. Introduced in 1885, it had smaller wheels, almost the same size. It had front-wheel steering and the rear wheel was sprocket-driven by a chain from a forward-mounted chain-ring. This made it possible to alter the gear ratio by changing the size of the sprocket and the chain-ring. Almost overnight the high-wheeler was obsolete. The bicycle as we know it today had arrived.

TOP *In 1885 James Starley launched the Safety Bicycle.*

ABOVE *The ordinary, or highwheeler, had a reputation for accidents.*

OPPOSITE *The bicycle track at the Vélodrome de la Seine, Paris, 1900.*

THE CYCLING BOOM

In the century since the early 'golden age' of the bicycle, it has had its ups and downs. In the more affluent societies the motorcar became the preferred mode of transport and the bicycle fell from favour. In some countries it became a social measure, because the working classes had to make do with a bicycle while the more affluent could afford motorized transport.

The recognition by some in the late 19th century of the fact that the bicycle provided a pleasant and easily practised form of exercise was largely forgotten. The bicycle had become a cheap form of transport for those who could not afford a car.

Competitive cycling continued to be practised by small groups of people who banded together in clubs and societies. It was largely ignored by the mainstream of society in most countries and viewed by some as an esoteric pastime pursued in obscure corners of the countryside.

Even in mainland Europe, where bicycle racing was the most popular sport, and its heroes almost gods, the large

RACING ACCELERATED THE TECHNICAL DEVELOPMENT OF THE MACHINE AS RIDERS SOUGHT MECHANICAL ADVANTAGES OVER THEIR RIVALS

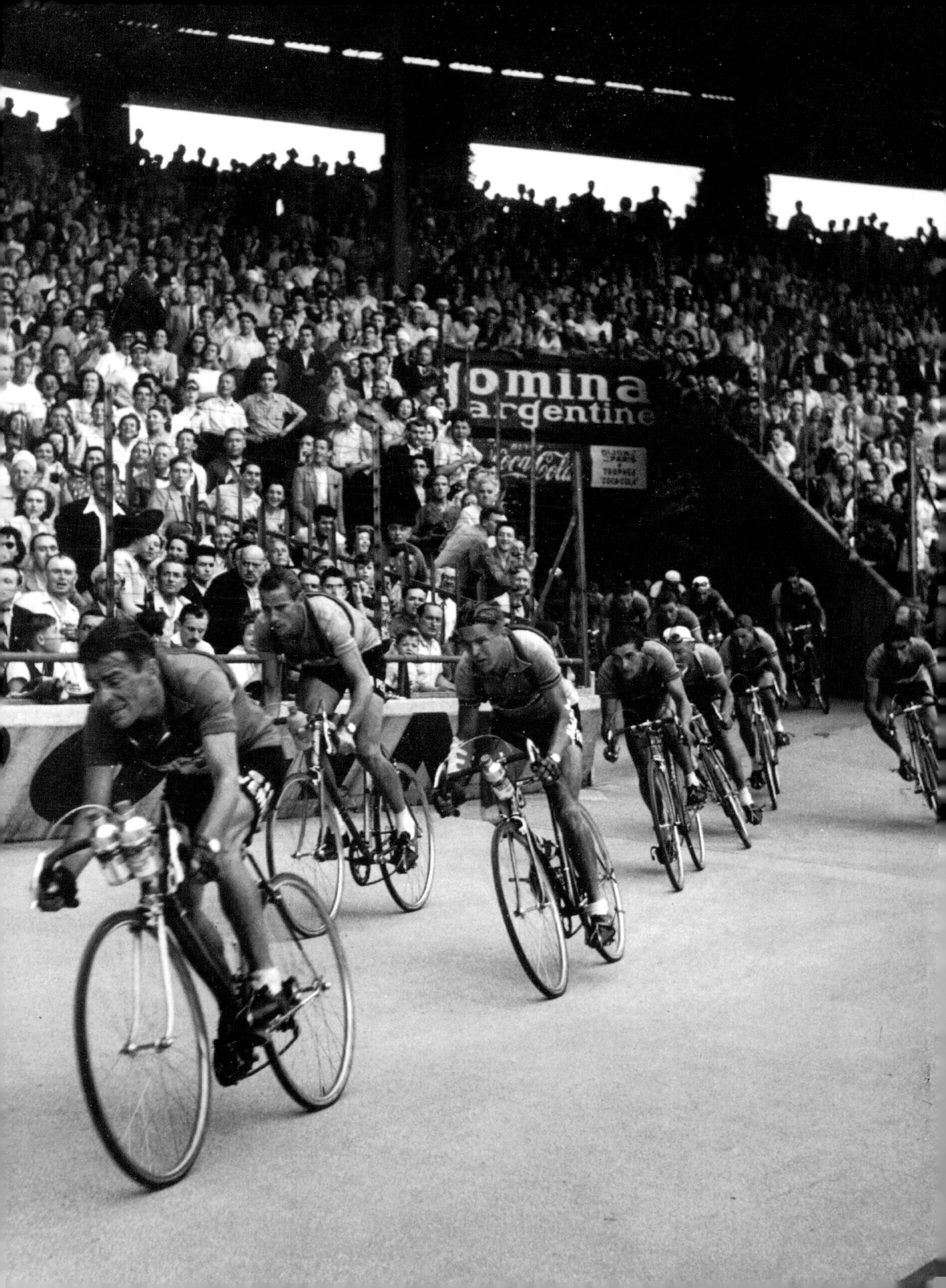
omina
argentine
Coca-Cola

middle ground of recreational cycling was the province of the arch enthusiast, better accepted than in the rest of the world, but still a minority. Fitness was seen only as a by-product of competitive sport and not as a desirable end in itself.

By the mid-1970s, there had emerged an increased awareness of the depletion of the world's natural resources, of air pollution, and the destruction of the environment. This resulted in the growth of bicycle sales. People also became more aware of the health benefits of regular exercise. There was a general movement toward taking greater care of the body. The pursuit of fitness came to be accepted as a normal social activity.

Other developments paralleled this movement. Competitive sport had become tougher, more professional and, increasingly, technology provided the edge that determined the winner, particularly at Olympic level. Cycling, partly an athletic sport, partly technological, became a focus for technical experimentation. There were experiments with almost every aspect of the bicycle and its rider. All this new technology attracted fresh interest in the bicycle.

By the end of the 1970s more bicycles were being sold in the USA than cars.

From the early 1980s America, the largest economy in the world, drove the technological revolution, aided by the industrial and manufacturing skills that came out of Japan and then Taiwan in the late 80s. Astonishingly, the bicycle became a desirable technological possession.

The beauty of it was that it was also a perfect method of gaining physical fitness. Socially the bicycle had made a comeback.

It did not take long for manufacturers, worldwide, to seize the opportunity to produce bicycles incorporating the new technologies, and to market them as technological playthings for affluent buyers.

At the same time, sporting promoters saw an opportunity to satisfy a need for events that would be attractive to this new breed of cyclist. Organized cycling began to change its focus. How it changed varied from continent to continent. What was consistent worldwide was the increase in the numbers of people riding bicycles for pleasure. Cycling boomed in the late Seventies and has never looked back. Although the bicycle trade throughout the world has had its periods of growth and recession since that initial boom, the trend has been ever upward and the choice of scientifically designed equipment available to the modern cyclist has grown.

WOMEN CYCLISTS

When 16-year-old Tessie Reynolds rode from Brighton to London and back in September 1893, wearing a trousered costume, she was lambasted by the British press: not only had she worn 'immodest and degrading' dress, she had used a bicycle with a top tube, had been paced unchaperoned by male friends, and had dared to ride strenuously: about 177km (110 miles) in 8½ hours.

Today there are other factors influencing women's choice of equipment, such as frame geometry and handlebar width (*see p56*) and the aim is greater speed and comfort, not less.

OPPOSITE *In Europe during the first half of this century, bicycle racing became the most popular sport and its heroes almost gods.*

ABOVE *Hélène Dutrieu was a star of French cycling and early aviator who received the Légion d'Honneur. Here she is shown riding a brakeless track machine, equipped with a Simpson lever chain, which was wrongly thought to give mechanical advantage over standard chains.*

SOME OF THE WAYS TO ENJOY YOUR BIKE

RIDING IN A GROUP

One of the surprises for newcomers to cycling is the aerodynamic benefit of drafting behind another rider or group of riders. This is why cyclists like riding in a bunch.

Riding close behind someone else reduces air resistance. This means that the rider at the back can travel at the same speed as the leading rider, but with less effort. Following a group of riders enhances this effect. A group of riders taking turns to lead and follow share this effect so that all the riders in the group benefit. This enables them to cover a route, either faster than if they rode alone, or with less effort. And what could be more sociable than enjoying refreshments at a stop after working together to get there?

Most clubs form where there are large concentrations of cyclists and for that reason are normally urban-based. Cycling clubs might have competitive racing as an objective, others are formed by riders who concentrate on touring, or on cyclo-tourist events.

For a novice the most important advantage in joining a club is to ride regularly with others. This provides a valuable opportunity to learn the techniques of cycling – from riding in a bunch to mending a punctured tyre.

TOURING

Soon after the development of the first bicycle, it became a vehicle suitable for touring the countryside. Many times faster than a human being can walk, it also uses less of the rider's energy resources, enabling a fit cyclist to cover great distances in the space of a day's riding. At the same time, it is slow enough for the rider to appreciate the vistas of the surrounding landscape.

Modern touring bicycles are fitted with specialized equipment developed specially for the task, such as lightweight panniers.

Most tourists tend to tour alone or in small groups, although there are tour operators who will take care of some of the chores of organizing accommodation, transport, foreign documentation and so on. They often provide back-up vehicles for luggage and mechanical service if needed, doing away with the need for panniers and luggage racks to carry one's daily needs.

There are also those sometimes referred to, unkindly, as credit card tourists. They tour on stripped-down bikes, carrying the minimum of spare clothing and relying on the purchase of food, accommodation and essentials at their overnight stopovers.

For the true tourist, however, there is an undeniable attraction in being totally independent and self-sufficient, even if it means carrying everything you need on the bicycle.

RIGHT *The racer, tourist, and cyclo-sportif do not under normal circumstances occupy the same road space.*

 # AIR RESISTANCE

Riding close behind another cyclist reduces air resistance. This means that the rider at the back can travel at the same speed as the leading rider, but with less effort. Following a group of riders further reduces the energy expended. A group of riders taking turns to lead and follow share this effect so that all the riders in the group benefit.

RANDONNEUR OR AUDAX?

Randonneur and Audax events originated in France, although the inspiration for them came from Italy as far back as 1896. In essence, the two are very similar. It is a form of competitive long-distance cycling.

The French term *randonneur* does not have a direct equivalent in English. Loosely, it refers to an outing, or a ramble, but for cyclists it has become a term to describe a cycling enthusiast who rides long distances under controlled conditions, striving to complete the distance inside a predetermined time.

The events are usually ridden over set distances, ranging from 200km (124 miles) to 600km (370 miles) without a support team. Apart from assistance available at *contrôles*, or checkpoints, along the way, the cyclist has to remain self-sufficient.

The competitor carries a card, called a *brevet,* that has to be stamped and signed at each *contrôle*. This card is then signed by the rider at the finish and handed in to the event organization. The event organizers check that each card is correctly signed and stamped and submit these results to a national administrator who reviews and approves the results. These results then go to the Audax Club Parisien (ACP) which acts as a controlling body for Randonneur events worldwide. The club certifies the results and issues the rider with a certificate, confusingly also called a *brevet*.

Despite the French influence and the ACP's control, it is a very international system – neither the rider's national affiliation nor the country in which he qualifies for a *brevet* has any bearing.

The difference between the Audax (the Latin word for bold) and Randonneur events is that in the Audax system, riders compete as a group. They ride together at a speed high enough to finish in the set time, but without leaving anyone behind.

In the Randonneur, riders take the route at their own speed, with or without the company of others. The French call this *allure libre* (free pace).

This is the only basic difference, and the end result – of happy, fit riders enjoying the camaraderie of the event – is the same.

Just to confuse matters, many Randonneur clubs and associations have the term Audax in their title – not least the international controlling club, Audax Club Parisien.

RIDING CENTURIES

In the United States and Canada, organized cycling developed through clubs providing their members with a goal that has become recognized throughout cycling in North America: this is to have ridden one or more 'centuries' in a day. The century refers to 100 miles (161km). Modern centuries generally provide the entrants with the choice of two or three different

distances, one of which is a 'one hundred mile' century. Even that is not always the case, because several events provide for metric centuries, that is 100km (62 miles), and at the other extreme there are also many double century rides of 200 miles (322km).

There are always riders for whom speed and time are important, or who enjoy competition, so that the event develops into groups who want to do the distance in the shortest possible time and those who just want to enjoy the ride.

Some riders will choose a leisurely ride through inviting countryside, coupled with

ORGANIZED RECREATIONAL RIDES PROVIDE A STRUCTURE WITHIN WHICH ENTRANTS CAN ENJOY THE SPORT IN THE COMPANY OF OTHER ENTHUSIASTS.

shady, wooded climbs and safe descents, while others might want a challenge that will push them close to exhaustion. The centuries, like other organized recreational rides, provide a structure within which entrants can enjoy the sport in the company of other enthusiasts.

CYCLO-SPORTIF EVENTS

Cyclo-sportif events have become a popular competitive event in Europe during the past 10 to 15 years. Similar to Randonneur events, cyclo-sportif rides are more closely related to road racing and often take place over the same routes as the famous races such as the Tour de France. Most riders attempt these events for the sense of achievement.

Perhaps the oldest cyclo-sportif event is the Marmotte in France, which was first organized in 1981. The attraction of this event is that it finishes at the Alpe d'Huez, famous for its mountain-top dramas during the Tour de France.

L'étape du Tour is perhaps the best known cyclo-sportif, with around 7500 riders competing over one of the mountainous stages of the Tour de France. Roads on the route are closed to other traffic as in the Tour de France itself and food and mechanical service are available to all competitors.

Usually, as with the 'centuries' in North America, the entrant can choose from several different distances. Cyclo-sportif events are run over routes that vary greatly in terrain and severity from one event to another. These events often make use of transponder technology to time the competitors.

A typical event frequently offers a computerized results service, mechanical back-up in case of breakdown, stops for food, marshals to control the traffic, and police escorts. As with any other bicycle race in Europe, the locals line the route to offer verbal encouragement.

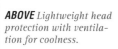

ABOVE *Lightweight head protection with ventilation for coolness.*
OPPOSITE *The scenic beauty of La Marmotte.*

GOLDEN BIKE SERIES

Initially based on four events in three European countries, the Golden Bike series was launched in 1999 by the world controlling body, the International Cycling Union (UCI). The aim of the series is to promote high-level and high-quality cyclo-tourist events, which are open to all. Events in the series now include rides in Belgium, France, Germany, Italy, the Netherlands, South Africa, Spain and Switzerland, although these change from

year to year. Any cyclist who has taken part in at least two foreign events (other than his/her home country) of the Golden Bike calendar is awarded a Golden Bike collector's jersey.

ROADIE CULTURE

For every professional rider or serious amateur taking part in an organized event, there are hundreds who simply enjoy getting out there on their bikes.

You don't have to be rated or timed to enjoy going fast on a lightweight road bike.

You could persuade a group of friends to join you for a cycling holiday based at a hotel somewhere in great riding country. Or you can join a club, affiliated to the national body (*see p137*) which may also give you the benefits of some form of insurance and legal aid and a programme of rides, (*see Organization of the Sport pp135–138*).

OPPOSITE *While many road bicycles are built and as complete ready-to-ride units, all of them are built up with components sourced from different manufacturers.*

CHOOSING A BIKE

The bicycle as we know it originated in 1885 with the introduction of the Rover Safety Bicycle. In its simplest form, the 'Safety' has changed little since then. The Rover had two wheels of almost equal size, driven by a continuous roller chain connecting two unequal-sized sprockets, designed to gear up the pedalling cadence of the rider. In appearance it was recognizably a bicycle as we know it today, more than 100 years later.

With the term 'general purpose bicycle' we have in mind a bicycle intended for use as a general means of transport. A vehicle intended for short errands and that might stand unused for long periods in the garage or shed. A bicycle suitable for this purpose can take many forms. Until recently it was generally the long-standing roadster design, very close to the original prototype of the Rover Safety.

More recently, though, it has been largely replaced by the cheaper, mass-produced versions of mountain bike. Simple, cheaply built, it serves the purpose as a vehicle for local excursions, short journeys, or for children to ride to school. Often it is their introduction to cycling.

ABOVE Top-of-the-range bicycle.

TYPES OF BIKE AVAILABLE

THE ROAD BICYCLE

The modern road bike is modelled after the road-racing bicycle that evolved in Europe. It was developed from bike racing and in particular the great stage races that demonstrated the huge distances that could be covered with a bicycle.

This bicycle has a lightweight diamond frame, drop handlebars, narrow wheels and derailleur-type multiple gear systems (*see p42*). It is normally built up with components from different manufacturers who specialize in the production of those components.

In technical specification and cost, it can vary from a cheap sports bicycle to a machine that would satisfy a competitor in the Tour de France. However, in general outline they all look similar.

A more detailed explanation of the various components that make up the modern road bicycle will be found in Chapter 4. While many road bicycles are built and marketed as complete ready-to-ride units, all of them are built up with components from different manufacturers.

It is possible to buy a frame set (a frame and fork), or even just a frame, from a frame builder and the other components from various other manufacturers. Many bicycles are customized in this manner to suit the individual rider.

The specification chosen by the rider depends on the intended use of the machine, personal preference, and the amount of money the rider is willing to spend.

This is the road rider's bicycle of choice, someone for whom the bike has become an extension of the self; the seven-league-boots that can take a mere human over the horizon in an hour or two; a vehicle that will provide an outlet for the competitive spirit; or an exercise machine with which to achieve physical wellbeing.

A TOURING BIKE

Serious tourists will have a road bicycle similar to the machine described above, built with out-sourced componentry and with the same opportunity to customize the bike to suit the purpose or the pocket.

However, because the tourist is likely to cover considerable distances over consecutive days and needs to carry most, if not all daily needs, the usual road bicycle specification is modified.

The frame is designed for more comfort on long rides, with shallower angles and a longer wheelbase providing greater comfort at the expense of performance.

It will often have special lugs or clips built into the frame, saddle or handlebars for specialized touring components such as panniers to carry tools, spare clothing and personal items; racks for camping equipment; handlebar-bags with map windows; and wet-weather equipment, including mudguards (or fenders).

As with customizing a road bicycle, a touring bike specification is often limited by financial considerations rather than imagination. A normal

MANY RIDERS USE THEIR MACHINES FOR DIFFERENT PURPOSES DURING THE YEAR. FOR THEM AN ANNUAL LONG-DISTANCE TOUR DOES NOT WARRANT THE EXPENSE OF A SPECIALIZED TOURING BIKE.

road bicycle can be adapted for touring. Many riders use their machines for different purposes during the year, and for them an annual long-distance tour does not warrant the expense of a specialized touring bike. The same bike will have to suffice.

Panniers can be fitted to most conventional road bicycles, as can handlebar bags and luggage racks. The specially built touring bike is simply more convenient and, over a long distance, more comfortable.

A MOUNTAIN BIKE

Mountain biking was an American innovation that surfaced in California in the early 1980s. Initially the bikes were modified roadsters or lightweight road bicycles. Experience and frequent breakages provided the impetus to develop a machine designed for its intended use.

The mountain bike today is built to withstand the rigours of recreational and competitive off-road cycling. A heavy gauge or reinforced tubing is used in the frame construction. Wide knobbly tyres, for better grip in soft and often muddy conditions, necessitate

more clearance between tyre and frame, which in turn dictate a different shape of frame and an alternate design of brake calliper.

Suspension systems have been developed for the front forks and the back wheel. Some of the more specialized machines are fitted with disc brakes for better braking in wet and muddy conditions.

Mountain biking, whether competitive or recreational, provides a different experience to cycling on the road. For many mountain bike riders, not having to share a road with motor vehicles is the deciding factor.

ABOVE LEFT *Mountain bike disc brake.*
ABOVE *A hi-tech modern mountain bike.*
LEFT *Mountain bike rear suspension.*

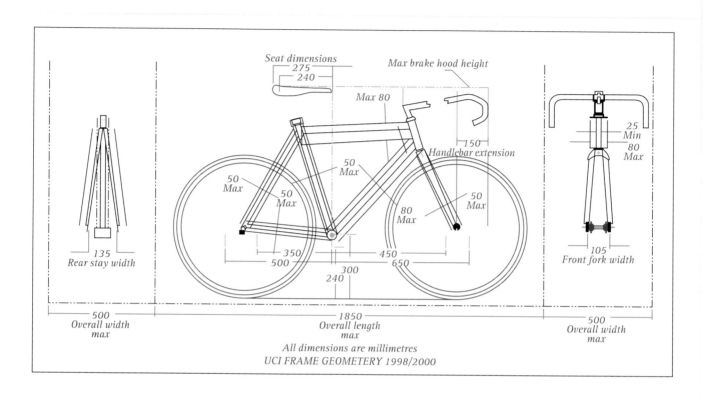

Seat dimensions
275
240

Max brake hood height

Max 80

150

Handlebar extension

50
Max

50
Max

50
Max

50
Max

80
Max

350
500

450
650

300
240

25
Min
80
Max

105
Front fork width

135
Rear stay width

500
Overall width
max

1850
Overall length
max

500
Overall width
max

All dimensions are millimetres
UCI FRAME GEOMETERY 1998/2000

ABOVE *The International Cycling Union's frame specifications.*

BELOW *Viacheslav Ekimov of Russia riding an aerodynamic (time trial) bike in the Tour de France 2003 prologue.*

SPECIALIZED MACHINES

There was much technical experimentation during the 1980s and early 1990s in the search for greater performance. Much of this development was applicable to the conventional road bike, but there were also trials with unconventional designs, particularly in the United States, few of which had any direct relevance to the road bike user or regular cyclist.

Time trialing and triathlons introduced the development of bicycles (as well as helmet design and clothing) in wind tunnels. Better aerodynamic design resulted: wide-spoke wheels, or solid disc wheels appeared, fitted to ultra narrow frames with handlebars tailored to force the rider into an aerodynamic crouch in an effort to present the smallest possible frontal area. This might be ideal for producing the best possible performance in a race against the clock, but totally unsuitable for a day on a club outing, or a tour along a mountain range.

The Union Cycliste Internationale (UCI), the cycling world's controlling body, feared that competitive cycling, primarily a physical activity, was in danger of becoming dominated by the manufacturer's technology. They drew up specifications governing the extent to which the bicycle could differ from what had been the norm for nearly 100 years. This brought back a more rational approach to the technical development of the bicycle. Nevertheless, much of the technology developed in the production of those extraordinary machines has had a spin-off in more efficient versions of the conventional road bicycle.

RECUMBENTS

Recumbent cycles, where the rider travels feet first, represent the first major divergence from the standard diamond frame design. You sit in a seat with support for the back and extend your legs forward. This position lowers the centre of gravity, which speeds up handling, and allows more powerful braking than on a conventional cycle. Certain designs of recumbent, may also offer greater aerodynamic efficiency and speed than a conventional cycle, especially when fitted with a fairing. Recumbent bikes are classified by wheelbase (distance between wheel axles), wheel size and position of the crankset.

DECISIONS ON COST

A simple general purpose bicycle can cost very little, a road bike somewhat more. The cost depends on the component mix and, perhaps, on the imported content in the bicycle of choice. It will also depend on the choice of material (for example titanium or aluminium) and the manufacturing process.

Once you have an idea of the type of road bicycle you want, you need to establish the price range you can afford. Keep in mind that the purchase of the basic bicycle, while the single most expensive part of starting up, is not the end of the spending. You will also need cycling shoes, a helmet and

ABOVE *Club members can offer mutual support, motivation and advice.*

BELOW *Aerodynamic wheels developed through testing in wind tunnels.*

ABOVE *Worldwide, good bike shops are run by knowledgeable enthusiasts.*

BELOW *Saddlebag.*

appropriate clothing. Browsing through catalogues, or in a local bike shop, will give you some idea of what you need to budget for. Consider those purchases as a part of the overall price of your first bike.

Within the constraints of your budget you need to decide what kind and make of bike you want, whether you want a made-to-order bicycle or will be happy with a standard over-the-counter machine. Your requirements will also depend on whether you dream of riding an Alpine tour through the Austrian Tyrol or a randonneur brevet across northern France, or whether you plan on riding in a club group on weekends (which is most likely your starting point). Once you have been cycling for a while, you may change your initial goals. However, regardless of your goals and budget, the bicycle you buy will be a sophisticated machine of very light construction.

NEW OR USED

Often, the saving on a good second-hand machine can make it possible to raise one's sights. However, not all bicycle dealers stock

CHOICE OF SUPPLIER

A visit to a suitable bike shop will always be more constructive if you already know how much you want to spend and what you intend to use the bicycle for. You can then be shown a range of machines suitable for your purpose in your price range.

Generally, good bike shops are run by knowledgeable enthusiasts, and their advice is mostly helpful. Find out which are the good, enthusiast-run bike shops in your area.

Read up beforehand on what each of the major parts of a bicycle does (*see Chapter 3*). What is its purpose? How does it operate? What sort of price would you pay, typically, for that part as a separate component? Get a feel for the range of components that are readily available, so that your chosen machine can be easily serviced and repaired. Using components that are no longer being manufactured can make service and repairs costly or impossible.

Avoid buying a bike from a shop that sells everything from bicycles to general hardware. In most cases they will not sell the type of bicycle you need if you are planning to participate in some form of organized riding. Equally, the highly specialized shop that deals only in a single manufacturer's products will not provide you with the entire range of options you need to consider – unless, of course, you have your heart set on a machine made by that particular manufacturer.

When talking to various bike shops, try to assess what standard of service you are likely to get if you made your final purchase from them. Ultimately, you need to acquire sufficient skills to be able to service or repair the bicycle yourself, but that takes time and requires the purchase of a variety of tools. Initially, you will need the support of someone who can service your bicycle, close to where you live or work so that it is accessible.

If you have a friend who is already doing the type of riding you have in mind, then take that person along on your first investigations. However, at the end of the process, the person who pays for the bicycle makes the final decision. Similarly, no matter how long you spend shopping around, the choice of supplier is a personal one and largely based on trust.

second-hand bikes. You are more likely to find them advertised in the local newspapers, cycling magazines and online. When you go to view a bicycle being sold privately, ask a cyclist who has some technical knowledge of what you are looking for, to accompany you. Otherwise repairs or component replacement may obliterate the savings made in buying second-hand.

BELOW *Water bottle and cage.*

BELOW *Spoked lightweight wheels such as these are used on many bikes at the high end of the market.*

BIKE ANATOMY & ACCESSORIES

CHOICE OF EQUIPMENT

The selection is wide, whether you are a beginner or experienced cyclist and whether you choose a complete bicycle or separate components. The price of similar items also varies greatly. For that reason it is important to familiarize yourself with the major components. Learn to identify the different materials and manufacturing techniques that affect the cost of components.

Once you have narrowed down the search by eliminating the components that are unsuitable for your application, and identified what you need in terms of quality and function, you can begin to decide on cost. If this is a determining factor, then you need to decide which of the components can be substituted with a cheaper alternative without compromising the final product. The following are guidelines to help you draw up the specifications for your new road bicycle.

Head tube

Top tube

Seat tube

Down tube

Chain stay

Seat stay

Bottom bracket

FRAMES

The basis of the machine is a diamond frame. This is generally built up of four tubes to which stays and forks are attached to support the wheels. Frames are produced in various sizes to suit the anatomy of the rider. The correct size is important for comfort and efficiency (*see Chapter 4*).

At the top of this frame is a pin (called the seat post) to support the saddle and a stem to hold the handlebars. Both are adjustable in the frame to provide the correct dimensions for the rider's anatomy. Frames were traditionally made of steel. However, there are more options today:

*   chrome-molybdenum low-alloy steels, which can be brazed or silver soldered
    *   aluminium, either butt-welded or built with lugs and then epoxy-resined
*   carbon fibre

ABOVE Diamond frame.
BELOW Handlebar stem.

*   titanium
    *   magnesium, though rare.

All these materials are tried and tested, each with its advantages and adherents.

It is difficult to see the differences beneath the paintwork, but the retailer will use whatever material the frame is made of as a selling tool. However, the more you know about what you are buying, the less chance that a sales pitch will see you buying the wrong item.

Manufacturing materials have a significant effect on the performance and cost of the frame. Before the 1980s, all quality cycle frames were manufactured of double-butted chrome-molybdenum steel tubes, brazed together with the aid of cast lugs that joined the tubes. This type of frame is still produced, and many riders will not use any other type of frame.

The cost of steel frames varies greatly. The justification for the differences in cost is not always immediately evident. Steel frames are often produced using straight gauge, seamed steel tubing. While far cheaper

than the double-butted chrome-molybdenum tubing used in higher quality frames, it produces a heavier, less responsive frame. Variations in the grade of chrome-molybdenum tubing also accounts for differences in cost.

Alternative materials began to erode the market share of steel frames from the early 1980s. Aluminium frames, built from seamless aluminium tubes, joined by cast lugs bonded with high-tensile adhesives, soon became an option. The Italian manufacturer, Alan, initially led the way in the production of ultra-light frames.

Titanium is sometimes used for lightweight frame manufacture. However, costs, and the difficulties of welding this material, prevented it from taking a meaningful share of the lightweight bicycle market.

Carbon fibre has many advantages even when shaped into tubing, but a straight copy of the design of the metal bicycle does not make best use of this material. It would appear that the most efficient design for composites is a monocoque, where the entire frame is a single piece. However, to date monocoque designs are limited to use in racing and the upper end of the market.

As an offshoot of motor racing technology, frames were cast in one piece from the same plastics. However, it cost far more than an equivalent frame built by traditional methods, and the first of these was not a success.

Today manufacturers offer bicycles built of mixed materials, such as a mix of an aluminium alloy bonded with carbon fibre or other plastic materials to produce a rigid, but light frame at a competitive price. This has widened the choice of frame sets available.

Careful consideration of your intended use of the bicycle is essential if you are to get the best value for your money.

HANDLEBARS

Drop handlebars, as used by racing cyclists, are first choice on a road bike, although some tourists prefer a straight handlebar similar to those on mountain bikes. Handlebars come in various widths. The width should match the width of your shoulders and should always be fitted to a stem of appropriate length.

ABOVE AND LEFT Drop handlebars.

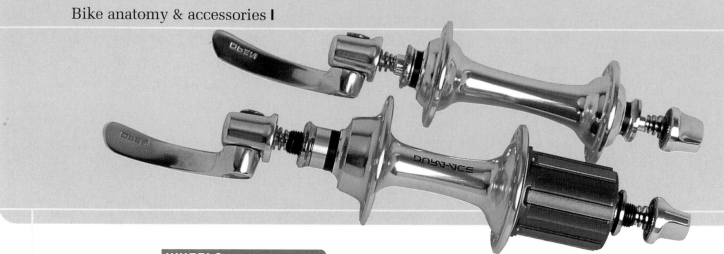

WHEELS

The wheels, although the same size, are not interchangeable because the rear wheel has a wider hub than the front to permit the fitting of the drive sprockets. Wheels have three main components: the hub, the rim, and the tyre.

THE HUB

Wheels are built up of wire spokes radiating from a central hub containing an axle, supported by bearings and with some form of mechanical

TOP Front and rear hubs.

RIGHT The quick-release lever closed (top) and open (right).

fitting to attach it to the forks of the frame. This can be a simple nut, but the modern recreational bicycle has quick-release hubs front and back. This mechanism allows the removal of the wheel from the frame without tools, by the movement of a lever operating on a small cam.

High quality hub sets usually have sealed roller bearings, but quality hubs with ball bearings will do the same job adequately. However, they need more frequent servicing. Ball bearing hubs can give many years of service on touring bikes. Often this choice is dictated by your budget.

THE RIMS

There are two basic types of wheel: clincher and tubular.

Clinchers are also called high-pressure (HP) wheels and their tyres sometimes referred to as wire-ons or wire-beads.

Tubulars, used by racing cyclists, are also called sprints and their tyres referred to as sew-ups.

The edges of tubular tyres are sewn together to encase the inner tube. A tubular rim

(sprint rim) has a slightly concave, smooth top with no lips and the tyre is held in place with glue or shellac. In case of a puncture, a complete tubular tyre can be replaced very quickly, an advantage when racing. However, mending a puncture on a tubular is time-consuming.

The more common clincher (HP) rim takes either a tubeless tyre or separate tyre and tube. It has an open casing, the two edges of the casing nestling within the lips of a U-shaped rim. The edges are reinforced with beads of wire or nylon to retain shape and stay inside the rim when the inner tube is inflated.

Most bicycles have clincher rims. They are built with spokes, usually stainless steel, because chrome spokes are slightly more prone to breakage.

There is a wide variation in rim depth, with deep aerodynamic section at one extreme, to flat rims with a very slim section at the other.

The reason for variation in rim depth is that the deeper the rim the more it reduces the last 50–60mm (2–2½ in) of

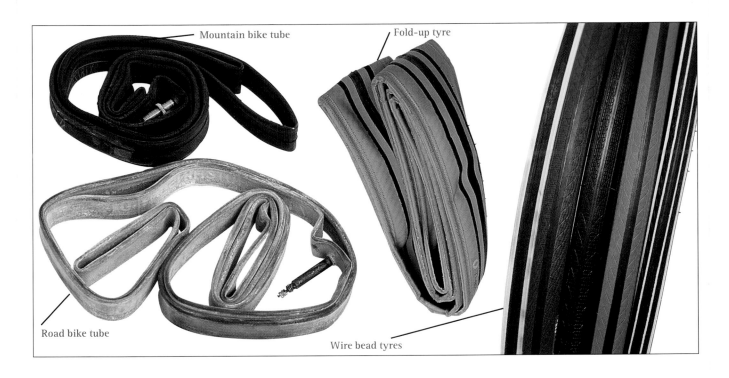

Mountain bike tube

Fold-up tyre

Road bike tube

Wire bead tyres

spoke. This is the part of the spoke which generates the most wheel drag as it reaches the highest relative velocities. This drag can be reduced by increasing rim depth to shorten the spokes, or by reducing the number of spokes, or both.

Built-up spoke wheels on good aerodynamic rims generally have between 32 and 36 spokes, although rims using fewer spokes are also available. The most common spoke pattern is 36 spokes, front and back. The aerodynamic advantages of deep section rims are often negated by a more rigid, harsher ride and difficulty in riding in strong winds, particularly side winds.

TYRES

There are three distinct types of tyre suitable for fitting to a clincher rim. The first two require a separate inner tube rather like a motorcar or motorcycle; the third is tubeless.

- The most common are tyres with a wire inside the inner lip of the casing to act as a bead that fits into a matching groove or lip inside the well of the appropriate rim. The pressure exerted by the inflated inner tube then holds the rim bead firmly in position.
- The fold-up tyre is similar, but the bead is made of Kevlar® which serves the same purpose as the wire bead above. It is usually

lighter than the equivalent wire-beaded tyre and its flexibility means it can be folded up and carried as a spare. For general riding within a couple of hours of your starting point, it suffices to carry spare tubes to ensure you get home in the event of a puncture.

ABOVE A selection of tyres and tubes.
BELOW Typical clincher (or HP) wheel with clincher rim.

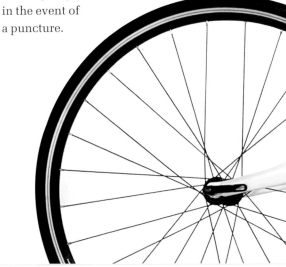

ABOVE Brake callipers.
BELOW Sealed
bottom bracket.

However, for longer distances, where there is no service within reasonable range, a fold-up is good insurance against a serious blow-out.

• The tubeless tyre is an airtight, hollow unit, with beaded skirts enabling it to be mounted on a clincher rim in the same way as the tyres described above. Inside the tyre is a fluid that hardens on contact with the outside air. In the event of a puncture the internal air pressure forces this fluid out through the hole and, in hardening, it seals the puncture. With small punctures it seals quickly enough to allow only a slight reduction in tyre pressure. If the puncture is more serious it might be necessary

to dismount long enough to pump the tyre up to pressure again. This technology has been spearheaded by Czech manufacturer, Tufo. The design is subject to patents. Some professional racing teams have been using tubeless tyres and they are available in most parts of the cycling world. Despite some teething problems, I believe this is the tyre of the future.

BRAKES

Side-pull calliper brakes, to the back and front, acting on the rim of the wheel, are the most widely used on lightweight bicycles. This design uses a cable, actuated from the brake lever on the handlebar, drawing the two arms of the calliper together, causing the rubber blocks on the inner faces of the calliper arms to apply retarding friction to the wheel rim.

Differences in cost usually reflect the quality of manufacture and detail in the refinement of the basic design,

rather than any enhancement in the fundamental design. However, remember that your safety often depends on this small item. If you are building up a bicycle from components, it is not wise to economize here.

DRIVE TRAIN
BOTTOM BRACKET

The bottom bracket consists of an axle running through a shell in the bottom of the frame, held in place by either threaded metal cups and ball bearings or by a sealed bearing unit. The chainset (also known as a crankset) is attached to this.

CHAINSET (CRANKSET)

The chainset consists of two cranks, to which two or three different-sized cogs (typically 53 and 39 teeth), called chainrings, are attached. These, in turn, are attached to arms on the right-hand crank by small threaded studs.

These chainrings provide ratios, typically giving high and low extremes of 53x12 and 39x25. There are great differences in quality that account for a wide price range.

ROLLER CHAIN

Connecting the different elements of the transmission system is a roller chain. The modern bicycle uses a chain which was developed from the roller chain patented by Swiss-born Hans Renold

in 1880. Renold's invention paved the way for the introduction of the Rover Safety Bicycle, which is the forerunner of the modern racing bike.

Modern chains are much thinner than those on the original Rover and, to assist the crude action of the derailleur (*see p42*), it has to be flexible. It is now made worldwide, and is often designed to suit a specific design of sprocket cluster.

FREEWHEELS

Today the cluster of sprockets is typically part of a cassette hub built into the wheel. The freewheel mechanism is built

into the hub and holds the sprockets (cogs). On the outer end of the hub is a splined or ribbed casing onto which eight, nine or ten sprockets are fitted, depending on the set-up you have purchased. These sprockets are locked onto the hub by means of a threaded small sprocket or by a special threaded fitment.

The advantage of this system is that it permits the replacement of individual sprockets, either because they are worn, or for the purpose of altering the series of ratios. For example, a cluster set-up of

DRIVE TRAIN

The parts of a bicycle that have to do with generating forward motion are in the drive train: pedals, cranks, chainwheels, bottom bracket, chain derailleurs, rear sprockets and rear hub. The drive train serves two functions: it transmits power from the source (your legs) to the wheels, and it varies the amount of torque. 'Power' is the rate or speed at which work is done and 'torque' is turning or twisting force. Gears help you achieve an efficient rate of turn.

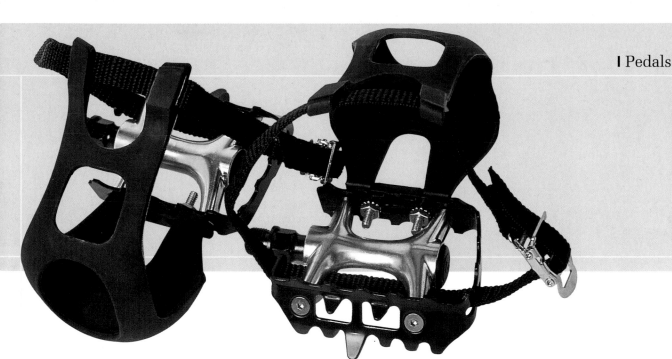

14- to 23-tooth sprockets can be replaced to give a range of 13- to 28-tooth sprockets for a tour with climbs requiring lower gear ratios.

PEDALS

Attached to each crank is a pedal for the rider's foot to transfer muscle power from the rider's legs to the chainset. This can be a simple platform or framed 'quill' pedal, requiring a toe-clip and strap to fix the rider's foot to the pedal or it can be the modern clip-in (or step-in) type.

Platform pedals support the shoe and may be used open, without attaching the shoe. Rubber platform models are the basic type used on utility bikes. They give the foot full support, can be used either way up and do not accept toe clips.

Cage-design platform pedals save weight by eliminating some of the platform area so that the sole of the foot touches only the cage sides. On long rides with inadequate footwear the cage sides may bite into the foot, causing fatigue and numbness. Most cage pedals will accept toe clips and straps.

The modern clip-in (or step-in) type of pedal marketed by companies such as Look® and Time® are a mid-1980s adaptation of a system developed for skis.

Step-in pedals require a special type of shoe, with a metal or plastic cleat on the sole. The pedal is matched to this cleat so that the foot can be pressed into a sprung grip, from which it can be released by twisting the foot sharply outward. Usually the degree of force necessary to do so can be adjusted.

Once positioned correctly the cleats ensure that the foot is fixed securely to the pedal, with the ball of the foot over the axle of the pedal for optimum pedalling efficiency. These pedals were a marked improvement over the spring-steel toe-clip and leather strap.

ABOVE *Pedals with clips and straps.*
BELOW *Clip-in pedals.*

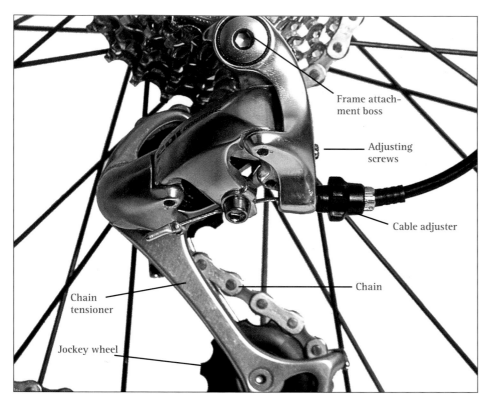

Frame attach-
ment boss

Adjusting
screws

Cable adjuster

Chain

Chain
tensioner

Jockey wheel

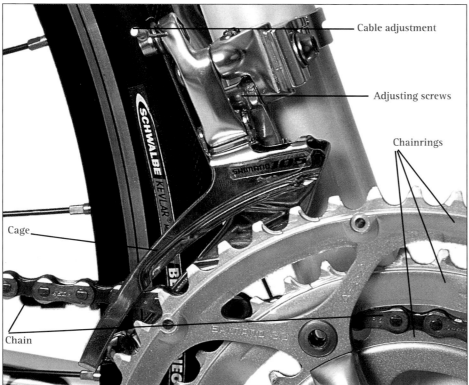

Cable adjustment

Adjusting screws

Chainrings

Cage

Chain

GEAR SETS

To vary the gear ratio it is necessary to move the chain from one sprocket to another. This is the purpose of the derailleur (the French word simply means 'de-rail-er' – because that is what it does). It appears to be a sophisticated piece of engineering, but is really just a crude, brute-force tool that levers the chain off one sprocket onto one adjacent to it.

A spring-loaded swinging cage ensures enough slack in the chain to accept the difference in diameter of different sprockets. The cage is attached to the parallelogram arms of the derailleur, through which an over-long chain is threaded. The spring-loaded cage holds the chain taut. To change ratios one has to move the parallelogram arms from side to side by means of a lever-operated cable (see *'gear-shifting levers' opposite*).

Derailleurs came into use in the early 1930s, particularly in central Europe where there are many long mountain passes requiring lower gear ratios than are commonly used on the flat. Development of multiple-gear systems continued over the next 25 years until, in the late 1950s, the first parallelogram action derailleurs came onto the market. By then the system had developed to where five-speed sprocket clusters could be accommodated, making

high-quality road bikes with 10 gear ratios possible. Today, with nine- and 10-speed clusters, 18- and 20-speed bicycles are the norm, and touring bikes are frequently fitted with triple chainsets coupled to eight-speed clusters providing a choice of 24 ratios.

The front derailleur is simpler. There is no need for a chain-tensioning cage, because that has been accommodated in the rear mechanism. It normally also needs only to de-rail the chain across two chainrings, occasionally three. The chain passes through a long narrow cage, which is fixed to a more compact version of the spring-loaded parallelogram arms used in the rear. It is also actuated by a lever and cable.

Gear-shifting levers mounted on the handlebars came onto the market in the early 1990s, largely replacing the system of separate gear levers mounted on bosses on the down-tube of the frame. They incorporate a 'squeeze into the handlebar' brake lever that can also be moved from side to side to operate the derailleurs. The left hand operates the front derailleur and the right hand the rear.

ABOVE *STI-type brake levers (see p67).*

OPPOSITE TOP *Rear derailleur showing the chain tensioning cage. This is a long cage suitable for a wide range of gear ratios.*

OPPOSITE BOTTOM *Front derailleur, showing its position in relation to the chainrings.*

Choose a good quality synthetic or leather saddle that fits your anatomy. The 'sitting bones' (the two pelvic bones you feel when you sit down on a hard surface) need to be supported. The saddle should not be so narrow that your body weight is borne by the fleshy part between those two bones.

Special saddles that are anatomically correct for the wider female pelvis are available. These may also have a deep groove or a split in the centre of the saddle to eliminate pressure on sensitive tissue.

SADDLES

The saddle, affixed to the saddle-pin (or seat post), comes in many variations of the basic triangular shape. Its 'fit' to the rider's anatomy is crucial to riding comfort.

TOP Woman's saddle.
CENTRE AND RIGHT Typical road racing saddle.

ACCESSORIES

High-pressure, continuous two-way-action mini-pumps can be clipped onto the side of a bottle cage. The normal length pump, also available in two-way action, provides a more comfortable (and faster) pumping action and will fit under the top tube, or in front of the seat tube. An inflator, with CO_2 cartridge, is faster than pumping and will fit in a saddlebag.

Most of the modern high-quality frames can be fitted with two water-bottle cages. Two pre-threaded inserts on the frame will accept simple hex-head or Allen-key fitting screws. Using both bottle cages does mean that you cannot place your pump in front of the seat tube, which may account for some of the popularity of the mini-pump.

Cycle computers that give information such as distance travelled, time elapsed, current speed, average speed and total distance covered are available in many variations.

Handlebar-mounted heart-rate monitors are available to help monitor training programmes.

A useful accessory is the wedge-shaped mini-saddlebag that is attached under the saddle with Velcro® straps. Tucked away beneath the rider's seat, it is large enough to take two spare tubes, a pair of nylon tyre removers and a small puncture repair kit.

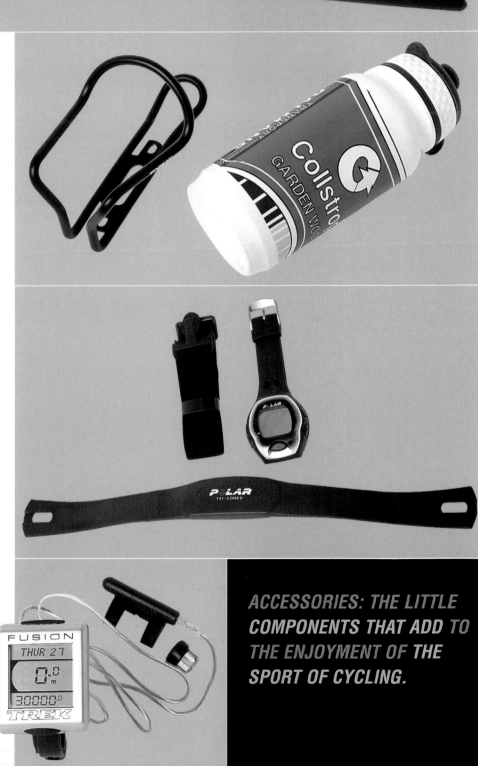

ACCESSORIES: THE LITTLE COMPONENTS THAT ADD TO THE ENJOYMENT OF THE SPORT OF CYCLING.

❯ CLOTHING

Cycling as a sport is made attractive by the bright clothing, machines and accessories of professional racing that receive worldwide publicity.

Clothing is colourful, usually lightweight, and specific to the activity. It can vary from a lightweight pair of Lycra® shorts and short-sleeved cycling jersey, to thermal tights, coupled with a nylon-faced long-sleeved top over thermal underwear and gloves – depending on the climate and the season.

Most modern recreational riders follow the fashions set by the professional racing cyclists, often adapted to suit local weather conditions. The lightweight 'road-racing vest' with full front zip and pockets across the lower back is convenient for many forms of cycling apart from competition. Equally, the shorts, designed to provide the professional with comfort under the most arduous conditions, cannot be bettered.

Riding shorts are generally tailored to fit like second skin. They have either a chamois or similar synthetic pad built into the inner crotch area of the shorts to provide protection in the area of contact with the saddle. This comfort is very important when riding long distances.

Racing jerseys and cycling tops are generally made of Lycra® or similar material which makes for a garment that is lightweight and close-fitting to reduce chafing. Many riders like the colour and fun of wearing replicas of professional racers' jerseys, but this style of top is also available in plain colours. For safety reasons it is advisable to wear another garment under the cycling top. A second layer of clothing will help reduce 'road rash' by

 # FASHIONS

Most modern recreational riders follow the fashions set by the professional racing cyclists, often adapted to suit local weather conditions. The lightweight road-racing vest with full front zip and pockets across the lower back is most convenient for many forms of cycling other than competition. Equally, the shorts, designed to provide the professional with comfort under the most arduous conditions, cannot be bettered.

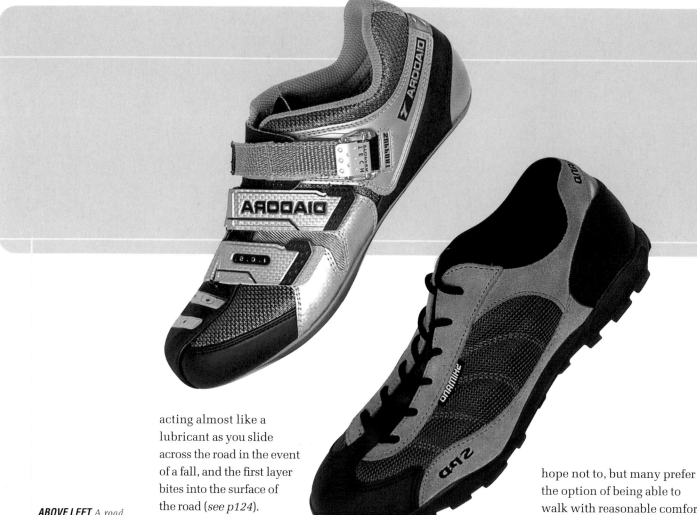

acting almost like a lubricant as you slide across the road in the event of a fall, and the first layer bites into the surface of the road (*see p124*).

Thermal jackets are a necessity in many parts of the world during the colder months, although opinions on what is 'cold' may differ between Sydney, Vancouver, London and Athens. Even in warm climates a long-sleeved over-jacket of some description is a necessary item of clothing. However, in climates where the winters can bring temperatures low enough for snow or ice, a good long-sleeved cycling jacket made from a thermal material is essential.

SHOES

Cycling shoes made for competitive road cyclists are designed for optimum performance, but not for walking. Of course, most cyclists don't expect to have to walk, or hope not to, but many prefer the option of being able to walk with reasonable comfort if their ride is more leisurely and includes time off the bike to do sight-seeing. One option is to use mountain bike shoes with recessed cleats in a shoe designed for walking and riding. However, this type of shoe is not as rigid as the conventional road cycling shoe and leads to tired feet during a long ride. The cleat used on mountain bike shoes also requires a different type of pedal.

Another option, often reverted to by touring cyclists, is to secure the feet to the pedal with toe clips and straps, so that they don't have to wear shoes with cleats.

The modern cycling shoe, designed for competition, provides an efficient link for the transmission of muscle power from the rider to the rear wheel. The shoe typically has

a very rigid sole made of plastic or composite material such as carbon fibre. Built into this sole are fitments for the cleats required by the rider's choice of clip-in pedal. The upper is normally of synthetic fabric, often with panels of mesh fabric to provide a 'breathable' covering for the foot. Closure of the shoe is generally with Velcro® fastenings in two or three cross straps. These shoes are available in a variety of colours.

TIGHTS

Colder climates often require some form of leg covering and tights are generally the most practical. Modified, close-fitting ski pants are also a practical option, but in either case the rider would wear normal cycling shorts underneath the outer layer to retain the comfort of the padded seat.

MITTS (GLOVES)

Cycling gloves are normally fingerless, have reinforced palms and lightweight fabric backs. This makes it possible for the rider to continue to carry out small tasks by touch, a factor often lost when wearing a full glove. The reinforced palm provides protection from road shocks transmitted through the handlebars and protection for the palms in the event of a fall. In cold weather, however, it is almost essential to wear long-fingered gloves.

WARMERS

Arm, knee and leg warmers can be adjusted for temperature easily on a ride by pushing them down and pulling them back up as required.

RIDING POSITION

Setting up an ideal position on a bicycle is time consuming and often arrived at by trial and error. Many professional cyclists, having achieved a position that works for them, will record every measurement needed to replicate that position and will ensure, when a bike is prepared for them, that it conforms to these measurements.

When a cyclist's position on the bicycle is set up correctly, the bike is propelled more efficiently and with greater personal comfort. The rider's body is relaxed and bike-handling improves. It is possible to pedal with more power, and yet the effort comes more naturally and easily.

New riders are given a great deal of conflicting advice, usually well-meaning, but which often results in a less-than-perfect position. Many would-be experts will offer formulae on frame sizing and positioning of saddle and handlebars, most of which may come close to an acceptable position, but seldom take into account the variations in body shape and proportion from one individual to another.

There are computerized systems touted by their designers as providing the perfect position for each individual. Books and innumerable magazine articles have been written on the subject. Most of them have something to offer, even though they may seem contradictory.

One thing that none of these systems and formulae do, however, is provide the perfect position for you.

This chapter will not tell you how to set up your bike perfectly. It will tell you how to set it up close to perfection, after which a little tweaking will achieve a position that takes into account the little idiosyncrasies of your personal physical make-up. You will arrive at this by trial and error as you gain experience, often with the help of an experienced coach or bike mechanic.

Seat post

Saddle adjustment

Frame size in cm/in.

ABOVE *How frame size is measured.*
BELOW *A racing saddle.*

FRAME SIZE

The size of the frame of your bike is expressed in either centimetres or inches. A 60cm (24in) frame is large and would be suitable for a tall rider, while a 48cm (18in) frame is small and would fit a very small rider. Someone whose legs are short relative to total body length would need a smaller frame than someone of similar height, but with relatively longer legs. Women tend to have shorter legs relative to total body length and so tend to use smaller frames than men of similar height.

Before looking at how to determine the size of frame that will suit you, we need to look at some of the other dimensions of the complete bike and examine how these affect riding comfort.

SADDLE HEIGHT

Saddle height is the measurement from the pedal to the top of the saddle, with the pedal at the bottom of its turning circle. This distance must relate to the distance between the heel of the foot and that part of the crotch that has contact with the saddle – your inside leg measurement.

You will need some help to measure your inside leg length. Stand, without shoes, with your legs about 25–30cm (10–12in) apart, then place a book between your legs so that the book spine is hard up against your pubic bone. Measure from the top edge of the book straight to the floor. This is the inside leg measurement, sometimes also referred to as pubic bone height.

When the pedal is at the bottom of the pedal stroke, the rider's legs should not be stretched out, but have a slight bend at the knee. The most popular means of determining the correct saddle height is to

set it at 109% of the inner leg length. This was ascertained as far back as 1967 by Hamley and Thomas, and has stood the test of time. The extra 9% of the inner leg length allows for the extension of the ball of the foot below the heel and will still allow a degree of bend in the knee.

Modern shoes affect this rule though, because they often have much thicker soles than those commonly worn in the late 1960s. Add to that the height of cleats attaching the shoe to the clip-less pedal used today. Following the Hamley and Thomas rule would then result in the rider's leg having slightly more bend in it than is ideal. To correct this, set the saddle at 109% initially and then raise it by the thickness of the sole of the shoes you are using. You will in any case make further minute adjustments to this in the search for the perfect position.

KNEE POSITION

Another position to be taken into account is that of the knee relative to the pedal. With the pedal crankarm in the horizontal position, a plumb line placed in the centre of the knee joint should be vertically above or slightly behind the axle centre of the crankarm.

I like it slightly behind the centre of the pedal, because in that way, the down-stroke helps you maintain your position on the saddle. If the knee is directly above, or slightly in front of the axle centre of the pedal, you tend to pull yourself forward when riding hard.

The right riding position lets your leg muscles work through the most powerful part of their range.

ABOVE LEFT Saddle height is the measurement from the top of the saddle to the pedal at the bottom of its turning circle. This height is determined by calculating your inside leg length.

CENTRE A plumb line from the centre of the knee joint should be vertically above, or slightly behind, the axle centre of the crankarm when it is horizontal.

RIGHT The correct degree of bend in the leg when the pedal is at the bottom of its turning circle.

45 º

REACH

Reach is the distance between the cyclist's shoulders and the top of the brake lever hoods, where the rider would place his hands when riding at a comfortable pace.

Reach is affected by the length of the frame's top tube. The seat tube and the top tube are usually the same length, but if your upper body is particularly long you might need a longer top tube, and the converse is true if you have a short upper body and long legs. Reach can be adjusted by changing the length of the handlebar stem.

The correctly adjusted reach will also allow the rider, when riding with the hands on the top part of the handlebar, or on the top of the brake lever hoods, to maintain the upper body at about 45° from the perpendicular. This will permit unrestricted breathing and enable you to see ahead better. This position also reduces strain on the neck and shoulder muscles.

Reach from shoulders to handlebars and saddle height are considered the two most important elements of the rider's position.

Whatever formula you use to set the basic position, it is the final, small personal adjustments that will provide you with the perfect position.

ABOVE *Keep your back at 45° above horizontal.*
OPPOSITE TOP *Reach, shown with hands on the brake hoods.*
OPPOSITE BOTTOM *Reach, shown with hands 'on the drops.'*

FINAL FIT

The bicycle can be adjusted to fit in with your personal dimensions almost irrespective of the length of the seat tube or the top tube.

The length of the seat post can be adjusted for saddle height. Equally, the length of reach can be adjusted by changing the length of the handlebar stem, and/or raising or lowering the handlebars in the frame.

Obviously, there are limitations to how far these adjustments can be taken. Even with the saddle pin pushed down as far as it will go into a 60cm (24in) frame, a short rider would still be unable to reach the pedals when sitting in the saddle. Conversely, a tall rider seated on a 48cm (18in) frame would need an abnormally long seat post, and would be unable to raise the handlebars sufficiently.

It is better to choose a frame size that requires minimal adjustment of handlebars and seat post to achieve a near-perfect position.

FRAMES FOR WOMEN

There are now, in most countries, manufacturers who offer competition-ready bikes designed around women's anatomy. Ask your retailer for a women's geometry bike. Apart from the different leg to overall height ratio (*see p52*), women also tend to have shorter arms than men of equal height. This can mean that the reach (*see p54*) on many standard sports bikes is too great for a woman. Women also have proportionally smaller hands and feet.

As a result the average woman will need a bike with shorter overall 'cockpit' length (handlebar-to-seat measurement). This can be achieved by a shorter top-tube length and/or by fitting a shorter handlebar stem (*see pp52–55*). Also, smaller hands need short-reach brake levers; narrower shoulders need narrower handlebars, and shorter legs spin more efficiently on shorter crankarms.

However, as the frame size gets smaller the wheelbase gets shorter. In extreme cases the front wheel can get so close to the bottom bracket that the rider's toes overlap the wheel and can touch if the front wheel is turned to the side. One solution is to lessen the angles of the frame, but that affects the 'feel' of the bike. Another is to fit shorter cranks. A third option is to build a frame scaled down to suit smaller wheels – usually 600s in place of 700s.

RIGHT *The saddle should be slightly higher than the handlebars.*

HAND POSITIONS

Ideally, the top of the handlebars should be slightly below the level of the top of the saddle. When riding with hands on the brake hoods, or on the top part of the handlebar, the hands should not support the full weight of the rider's torso.

A fairly pronounced bend in your elbow will help absorb road shock, while a near-horizontal forearm also helps, and places very little weight on your hands.

If the handlebars are too low it can cause discomfort in the lower back and between the shoulder blades. With a frame that is much too small, it is almost certain that the bars will be too low.

ABOVE LEFT Hands on the drops.
ABOVE RIGHT Hands on the tops.
LEFT Hands on the hoods.

LEFT *Richard Virenque of France descends the Col do Galibier during stage eight, from Sallanches to L'Alpe d'Huez, of the Tour de France.*

The curve of dropped handlebars is designed so that the rider is given three distinctly different positions in which to place the hands:

- The hands grip the brake lever hoods. They are designed for this and should be positioned on the bend of the handlebar so that the hands can grip them comfortably.
- The hands grip the top, straight portion of the handlebar (tops).
- The hands are inside the curve of the dropped, horizontal portion of the handlebar.

On long rides cyclists often suffer from pain in the palm near the wrist, or from numbness of the hands. This can be alleviated by wearing suitably padded riding gloves, or mitts, but also by frequently changing the position of the hands on the handlebars during a ride. Thicker bar tape will also help.

RIGHT Optimum position will ensure maximum transfer of power from the legs to the crankarm via the foot.

BELOW The cleat should be adjusted so that the centre line of the shoe is at right angles to the pedal axle.

BOTTOM RIGHT Clip-in pedal.

FOOT TO PEDAL

The position of the foot on the pedal is mainly determined by the adjustment of the shoe cleats. The ball of the foot should be exactly above the centre of the pedal axle. This is the optimal position for maximum transfer of power from the legs to the crankarm via the foot.

If the cleat adjustment places the ball of the foot slightly in front of the pedal axle, the efficiency is reduced. The advantage of the slightly more forward position of the foot is that it provides the foot with greater stability on the pedal, and reduces tension in the muscles and tendons of the lower leg. This position makes turning a higher gear a little easier and therefore it is sometimes adopted by racing cyclists for time trials. For most cycling, however, the ball of the foot should be placed directly above the centre line of the pedal axle.

The cleat should also be adjusted so that the centre line of the shoe is at right angles to the pedal axle, placing the foot directly in line with the bicycle's direction of travel. If the rider has a pronounced natural splay of the foot in one direction or another this might be uncomfortable, in which case some deviation from this might be necessary. However, any deviation to the left or right leads to a less efficient pedalling style.

FINALLY, BACK TO FRAME SIZE

Having taken into account each of the dimensions and adjustments that affect the ideal riding position, how do you finally decide what size of frame will suit you best?

To find the right frame size for a road bike, take your inside leg measurement (*see under Saddle Height p52*) and multiply by 0.65. This number gives you the frame size as measured along the seat tube from the centre of the crank axle to the centre of the top tube. Now you can go out and buy a frame that will permit you to set up a position that is close to perfect. The rest is up to minute adjustments, patience and time.

ABOVE A well-appointed workshop.
OPPOSITE By learning to do basic repairs yourself, you won't be stranded next to the road.
BELOW Washing your bike regularly helps identify areas of wear that may need attention. It also reduces wear on moving parts.

MAINTENANCE & REPAIR

GENERAL MAINTENANCE

If you are a less than average mechanic, then maintaining your bike can be left to a local cycle shop. More sensibly, you can learn to do basic maintenance and repairs yourself. However, once your new bike has been assembled by the dealer and your riding position has been set up, the bike should only require minor attention for the first few months of use.

If you ride almost every day, with long rides at the weekend, it will benefit from a service every two to three months. On the other hand, if your bike is only ridden occasionally, or just at weekends, then a service every five to six months will suffice.

You need to get into the habit of a regular cleaning routine for your new bicycle. Wash it regularly; this is an ideal way to identify any damage or wear that needs attention.

1. Tyre levers
2. Link extractor
3. Chain whip
4. Crankarm remover
5. Wheel spanner
6. Combination pedal/
   headset spanner
7. Cluster remover
8. Cone spanners
9. Pump
10. Lubricant
11. Solution (rubber cement)
12. Patches
13. Cable cutter
14. Combination
    hex wrenches
15. Combination
    pen knife
16. Combination
    hex wrench tool
17. Multi-tool

LEFT *Cleaning and lubricating the chain and sprockets will reduce wear.*
BELOW *A selection of sprockets.*

After each wash, once you have dried the bike, lubricate the chain, as washing will have removed much of the lubricant. An aerosol lubricant such as Q20, or any suitable PTFE- or Teflon-based product is fine. Avoid oil-based lubricants, or putting too much of any lubricant on the chain, because it attracts dust and grit. These combine with the excess oil on the links to form a fine grinding paste. This, of course, will accelerate wear to the chain and the chainrings. Also, the residue gets deposited on the bike frame, which then always seems to look mucky.

TOOLS

If you want to do the simple jobs yourself, you will need a few simple tools.
- set of Allen keys (hexagon wrenches)
- small flat- and star-end screwdrivers
- link removal tool
- pliers
- small ring/flat combination spanners
- cone spanners
- spoke key
- pedal removal spanner
- spray lubricant
- light hammer

Many of these tools come in combination sets that can be carried on a long ride.

CHAIN AND SPROCKETS

The chain, as well as the sprockets on the rear wheel cassette, can last very long, but not indefinitely. The sprockets that make up the cassette will last longer if the chain is changed frequently. If the chain and sprockets are allowed to gradually wear out together, you will end up having to replace both components once the chain starts jumping on one or more of the sprockets.

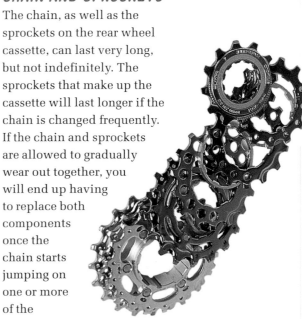

A new chain will not run on a very worn sprocket. If, however, you change the chain at regular intervals, before it is so worn that it starts jumping, then the sprockets will not wear as quickly. Since the cluster of sprockets will usually cost more than the chain, it also makes better financial sense.

To remove the chain you will need a chain extractor, sometimes referred to as a rivet extractor or simply a chain tool. One link of the chain fits into the tool, which has a threaded pin that matches the pin holding the links together. By winding the threaded pin it pushes the pin that holds the two parts of the link together just far enough to allow the links to be disconnected. Refitting the chain is simply a reversal of the above process, using the same tool, but turning the chain over so that the pin is pushed back in.

In addition to general wear of the links and the roller at the

ABOVE *Chain link extractor.*
BELOW
A – cable adjuster
B – brake quick release

link-pin, chains also stretch. If you count the links of your old chain, and compare it to a new chain with the same number of links, you will find the old chain is marginally longer. This is caused by wear on the rollers and link-pins. About 3mm (⅛in) is the maximum stretch you can allow before changing the chain. But if you have let it wear by that much you will probably need new sprockets as well.

CABLES

Modern brake and gear cables have a plastic lining inside the outer spiral-wound sheath, making it unnecessary to lubricate the cable as the plastic liner eliminates friction between cable and sheath.

Check for fraying brake or gear cables. Fraying can occur near the cable adjuster or at any point where they emerge from the outer casing, particularly inside the brake lever hood, where they are not readily visible.

If the brake or gear cables do not move smoothly, but with some resistance, you may need to replace the cable. Make sure it takes only normal

pressure to apply the brakes; if not, this could signify a frayed or stiff cable.

It pays dividends to replace cables before they show any visible signs of fraying or wear. Replacement is relatively simple for brake cables and for down-tube-mounted gear-lever cables. (It is a little more difficult if you have the latest STI type of combined brake and gear lever. *See p67*) Usually, removal of the old cable demonstrates the route to follow in reverse when fitting the replacement.

A light spray of lubricant at regular intervals on the cables, inside the brake hoods, on the moving joints of the front and rear derailleur as well as on the moving parts of the brake callipers will help to keep them working smoothly. Once you have lubricated everything, wipe off any surplus lubricant.

BRAKE PADS

Replace your brake pads (also called brake blocks) when they begin to show noticeable wear. There should always be plenty of rubber left. All brake pads have either a slotted or a block-shaped pattern in the braking surface when they are new; they often have a line or notches in the moulding to indicate the point at which the pad should be replaced.

Some designs of pad, if badly worn, can damage the wheel rim. Another adverse consequence of incorrect adjustment of the pads in relation to the rim is that as they wear, part of the pad can come into contact with the wall of the tyre when braking and will damage the tyre.

Different makes of calliper brakes often have pads made to fit a particular model. So be sure that you know which make and model of callipers are fitted to your bike when you buy new pads.

GEAR ADJUSTMENT

Derailleur gears, despite their complex appearance, are quite crude mechanisms. All they do in principle is de-rail the chain by forcing it off one sprocket and onto the next. The problems encountered most frequently are:

- Failing to move the chain across onto the smallest or the largest sprocket on the rear wheel.

 In the late Eighties the manufacturer Shimano experimented with a combined brake-lever/gear-change mechanism, which was finally launched to the public in 1991 as the Dura Ace STI system, with STI standing for Shimano Total Integration. Subsequently other manufacturers (Campagnolo in particular) copied the idea, if not the actual system. By the time other manufacturers caught up, STI had become another of those trade names that are accepted as a generic term for anything doing the same job.

ABOVE A non-STI brake lever.
LEFT A selection of brake pads.

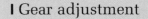 The STI type of combined brake and gear lever depends on an indexing system for the gear-change mechanism. Indexed shifting means that the shift control has click-stops that correspond to different gears. The length of the cable is adjusted so that the derailleur is in the correct position to correspond with each click-stop on the shifter.

Friction shifting, on the other hand, has a lever that moves smoothly through its range. The rider must learn exactly how far to move the lever to get from one gear to another. If the lever is moved too far, or not far enough, the chain will not line up with the sprocket, causing noise and roughness.

However, the length of conventional spiral-wound steel housing changes as the cable is bent, making adjustment difficult. So to get the best results from indexed shifting, a different type of cable sheath was developed by the Japanese company Shimano, since copied by most other manufacturers. This is a compressionless, or index-compatible cable housing, made up of straight wires running parallel to the cable and held together in a plastic sandwich. This type of housing doesn't change length significantly when it is flexed, but is not strong enough for brake cables.

ABOVE *Derailleur adjustment in the workshop.*

BELOW

A - top travel adjustment

B - bottom travel adjustment

C - cable indexing adjustment

- Dropping the chain off the chainrings when changing from the small chainring to the large one or vice versa.
- The chain rubbing against the front derailleur cage.
- Chain not engaging the sprocket teeth correctly and making a chattering noise.

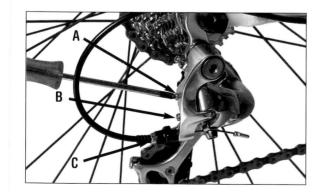

In the first three instances it is simply a matter of adjusting the travel of the mechanism. In the fourth instance, you need to adjust the indexing.

When making adjustments to the bike it is best to have the bike up on a work stand or on a wheel stand that will allow you to turn the pedals and the back wheel freely.

There are two basic adjustments: in and out travel of the derailleurs and, with indexed systems, centering the chain over the cogs (rear) and chainrings (front).

Turn the pedals and operate the gear levers to move the chain through the range of gears. Check that the gear

changes are quick and accurate. As you move the gear lever, the chain should transfer smoothly from gear to gear. If it will not shift onto either of the two extremities (largest sprocket and smallest sprocket at the back), then use a small screwdriver to turn one of the two small adjusting screws. These limit movement in opposite directions. Usually only very small adjustments are necessary to correct the fault.

Similar screw adjustments are possible in front. If the chain falls off the rings onto the bottom of the frame when you move the chain across from the big chainring to the small one, the movement of the derailleur cage toward the frame must be reduced. Similarly, if the chain falls off when changing up onto the big chainring, then the other adjusting screw should be adjusted to limit travel on that side.

The same adjustment of the front derailleur will usually stop the chain rubbing against the front derailleur cage. This rubbing usually occurs when the chain is at one of the extremes of either big chainring and biggest sprocket or small chainring and smallest sprocket.

The chain is designed to flex, because there are more sprockets on the rear wheel than there are chainrings at the front end. This means that the chain has to run diagonally, instead of parallel, to the line of its link plates for most of its operating life. However,

with 16 to 20 ratios to choose from, it should not be necessary to use the two extremes and most bike mechanics will recommend that you avoid using them.

Check the front derailleur cable for fraying and make sure that the chain cage is parallel to the chain. There should be a 5–6mm (³⁄₁₆–¼in) gap between the chain cage and the chainring.

When you work on the derailleur, always check the cable on the rear derailleur, near the cable anchor bolt, for evidence of fraying or damage to the cable. Wiggle the tensioner pulleys to see if they move about from side to side, indicating that they are worn.

If the chain clatters as it goes over the rear cluster of sprockets, and does not mesh correctly with them, it is usually the indexing that needs adjustment (*see p67*).

The shift control has click-stops that correspond to different gears. The length of the cable is adjusted so that the derailleur is in the correct position to correspond with each click-stop on the shifter.

The cable is drawn in or released in steps and this has to be synchronized with the position of the chain relative to the sprocket on which it is running. If the indexing is out of sync the chain will rub against the sprocket it is driving and make an annoying chattering sound. There is a knurled screw cable adjuster somewhere in the route of the cable from lever to derailleur. Sometimes it is on the downtube, or at the point where the cable connects to the derailleur. Either way, a small turn of the adjuster will correct the indexing and bring everything into sync again.

Many of these small adjustments become necessary due to a small amount of stretch in the cable.

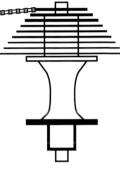

ABOVE *The chain is designed to flex. However, excessive cross-over like this causes wear and this gear can usually be obtained elsewhere in the range.*

BELOW *The position of the front derailleur.*

A HEAD-SET BEARINGS

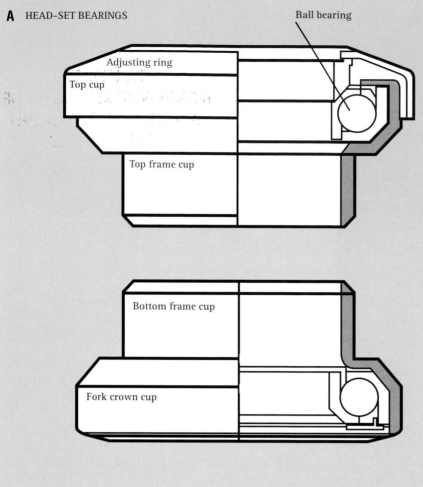

Ball bearing

Adjusting ring

Top cup

Top frame cup

Bottom frame cup

Fork crown cup

B BOTTOM-BRACKET BEARINGS

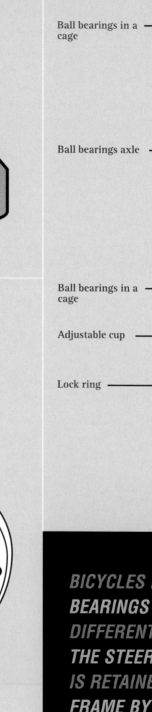

Fixed cup

Ball bearing shell in frame

Ball bearings in a cage

Ball bearings axle

Ball bearings in a cage

Adjustable cup

Lock ring

C HUB BEARINGS

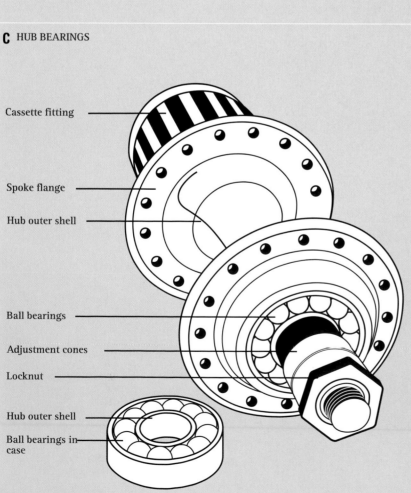

Cassette fitting

Spoke flange

Hub outer shell

Ball bearings

Adjustment cones

Locknut

Hub outer shell

Ball bearings in case

BICYCLES RELY ON BEARINGS IN A NUMBER OF DIFFERENT APPLICATIONS. THE STEERING FORK IS RETAINED IN THE FRAME BY TWO SETS OF BEARINGS.

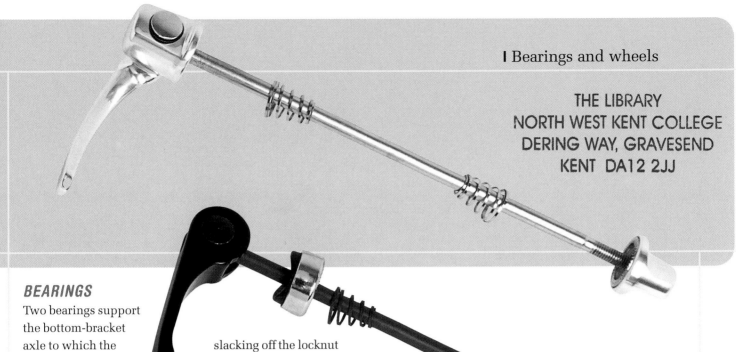

BEARINGS

Two bearings support the bottom-bracket axle to which the cranks and pedals are attached. There are also bearings in the pedals and in parts of the derailleur system.

The wheel hubs are, however, the most important. These may be either the cup-and-cone type with surfaces that can be adjusted for bearing play, or the non-adjustable cartridge type.

A sealed bearing is one which has rubber or plastic gaskets to prevent the entry of dirt. The term 'sealed bearing' is often used to refer to a cartridge bearing. This can be confusing because it is then not clear if someone is referring to a hi-tech cartridge-bearing unit, or a normal cup-and-cone bearing with a plastic dust cap.

In the basic cup-and-cone type of bearing system, the cone holds the ball bearing in the cup. To prevent the cone from moving, a locknut is tightened against the cone. If there is looseness from bearing play, the cone can be adjusted by moving it closer to the cup. Adjustment is done by slacking off the locknut and then adjusting the cone using a pair of very thin cone-spanners (or cone wrench), and then retightening the locknut.

WHEELS

Quick-release wheels have a hollow axle in the hub; this allows a skewer to go through the hub, on one end of which is a lever that operates a cam mechanism. On the other end is an adjusting nut. The cam places tension on the skewer and pulls the cam and the adjusting nut closer together, pinching the hub tightly against the fork-ends and holding the wheel securely to the frame. The adjusting nut controls the level of tension on the quick-release (QR) lever and cam.

In the event of a puncture, the wheel must be removed to effect repairs. If possible, begin by putting the bike in a bike-stand. If you are out on the road and no stand is available, the bike should be laid on its left side with the derailleur uppermost. Standing the bike upright without the rear wheel in place (and without a stand to support it) will put weight on the rear derailleur and probably damage it. Remove the wheels as follows:

• Release brake quick-release.
• Release the wheel QR by pulling outward on the lever of the QR skewer. If necessary, loosen the QR adjusting nut to clear any tabs at the bottom of the fork blades. This is a safety precaution on some bikes, designed to prevent a wheel from dropping out even if the QR is not closed.
• To remove the front wheel, guide the wheel down and out of the fork. For the rear wheel, first ensure that the chain is on the smallest sprocket, and then pull back on the rear derailleur to allow the sprockets to clear the chain. Lower the wheel, guiding it down through the brake pads and then forward out of the fork ends to clear the chain and derailleur mechanism.
• To replace the front wheel reverse the process,

TOP A closed cam quick release.
***ABOVE** An open cam quick release.*
OPPOSITE
A – head-set bearings
B – bottom-bracket bearings
C – hub bearings

ensuring that the QR lever is closed and the wheel is tightly in the forks.

- To replace the rear wheel, ensure that the wheel is the correct way round, with the sprockets on the derailleur side of the bike. Pull back on the rear derailleur to take up slack on the chain.

Guide the wheel up into the rear fork (also called the rear triangle), while at the same time ensuring that the chain engages with the smallest sprocket. Draw the wheel into the fork-ends. This sometimes requires a firm upward movement to ensure that the stubs of axle

on either side of the hub engage cleanly with the fork-end. Close the QR lever and check that the wheel is secured in the frame and that the wheel spins easily. Always adjust the quick-release lever so that it closes firmly.

ABOVE *Removing the rear wheel.*
RIGHT *Replacing the rear wheel.*

TYRES

The two main types of tyres are explained in Chapter 3 under 'Wheels' and 'Rims' (*see p36*).

The tyres on most lightweight bikes are those variously known as clincher, wire-on, or sometimes high-pressure (HP). For the purpose of this chapter, we will use the term clincher.

Racing cyclists prefer to use a tubular tyre or a 'sew-up' because it is lighter and more responsive, although clinchers have been developed so that this is no longer always the case.

The disadvantage of a tubular is that patching a puncture is time-consuming, because the tube is sewn up inside the casing. Repairing the puncture involves unstitching the casing and then restitching once the tube has been repaired. One has to carry a spare tubular – usually folded up and strapped under the saddle.

However, modern clinchers are often as light as any but the lightest tubular tyres – and of far greater convenience because the inner tube can be replaced or patched at the roadside if necessary. Consequently, even elite racers often make use of the clincher.

When a clincher is properly installed, it should run true with the wheel rim when the wheel spins. The line between the tyre's sidewall and the tread itself may have

some irregularity or waviness, but it won't affect the tyre's performance.

At regular intervals, each tyre should be examined for glass, small pieces of flint or other roadway debris embedded in the tread. Any such puncture risk should be removed before it can work through the tyre casing and perforate the inner tube.

If you've had to fix a puncture on the side of the road, don't reassemble the tyre and wheel before carefully feeling around the inside of the tyre. The cause of the puncture may still be stuck in the tread, waiting to puncture the tube again.

The inner tube has a valve known as a Presta. This type of valve requires that you unscrew a small knurled brass screw at the top of the valve stem before inflating the tube. When screwed down, this holds the valve stem in the closed position. The valve

may occasionally stick closed and prevent you from pumping up the tyre. To overcome this problem, unscrew the small knurled brass screw, fully depress the valve stem twice, releasing a small amount of air, which will free the valve.

Put your spare tubes, tyre levers, patch kit and any other tools in a sock or wrap them in a rag before storing them in your saddlebag. This keeps everything together and prevents tyre levers and tools from rattling.

ABOVE *A selection of modern clincher tyres.*
BELOW *Tyre levers.*

:: PUNCTURE REPAIR

TOP *Presta valve and knurled nut. Open the valve and let out any residual air.*

CENTRE *Wiggle the tyre to loosen the tyre bead from the inner part of the rim.*

RIGHT *Use a pair of tyre levers to lever the tyre bead up and over the edge of the rim.*

- If the puncture is small, letting the air out very slowly, then there may be some air left in the tube. This will make it difficult to get the tyre off the rim. Open the valve and release any residual air.
- Wiggle the tyre against the rim, pushing the sidewalls toward the centre of the rim. The tyre bead will have been squashed tightly against the inner part of the rim and you need to loosen it.
- Sometimes the valve will have a knurled locking nut holding the valve firmly to the rim. Remove this.
- Use a pair of tyre levers to lever the tyre bead up and over the edge of the rim. Do not use a screwdriver or other sharp implement as a lever. This can damage the tyre or tube.
- Insert one tyre lever under the bead of the tyre. Use a second lever 40–50mm (1½–2in) further round the rim. Then push both levers downward toward the spokes to lever a section of tyre off the rim. Clip one of the levers behind a spoke (there usually is a slot in the lever for this purpose). Remove the other lever and

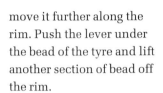

move it further along the rim. Push the lever under the bead of the tyre and lift another section of bead off the rim.

- Repeat the process until one side of the tyre is loose enough to remove the tyre from the rim. Usually, after levering off one or two parts, it becomes loose enough so that you can slide the lever along the rim, inside the edge of the tyre, to lift the side of the tyre over the rim in one stroke.

- Remove the inner tube from the tyre, starting opposite the valve. When you reach the valve, push the tyre away from the tube and lift the valve out of the valve hole. You can then remove the entire tube from the tyre.

- To make a thorough inspection of the tyre, it is best to remove it completely from the rim by levering the other side of the tyre over the edge of the rim. Check inside for cuts or damage to the carcass of the tyre, and for anything that might cause another puncture.

- Even if you do not remove the tyre completely from the rim, you should always

inspect it to ensure that the cause of the puncture doesn't continue to lurk in there to damage the new or repaired tube.

- Typically, after suffering a puncture out on the road,

you would replace the tube with a spare. One or two spare tubes can be carried in a small wedge-shaped tool bag that fits under the saddle.

ABOVE *Patches, solution and tyre levers*
LEFT (TOP) *Push the tyre away from the rim*
LEFT (BOTTOM) *Feel inside the tyre to ensure that the cause of the puncture is not lurking to cause another one.*

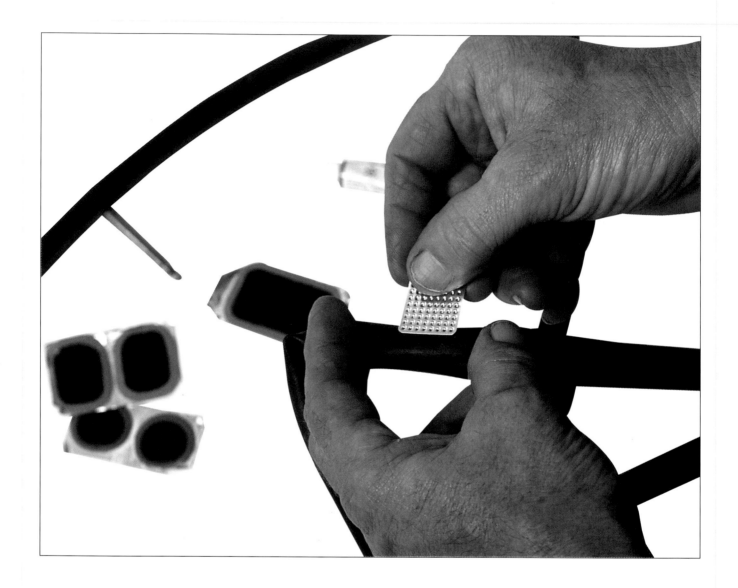

ABOVE Roughen the tube over the area of the puncture.

- If you plan to repair the inner tube at the roadside, try to find the air leaks by inflating the tube and holding it close to your lips or near your ear to feel or hear air escaping. Move the partly inflated tube full circle as you do so. If this fails to reveal the leak, then submerge the tube in water and look for escaping air bubbles.

- Roughen the tube with a piece of sandpaper or a stone in the area of the puncture.
- Take out a patch of an appropriate size and remove the backing to expose the shiny side of the patch.
- Put a small dot of solvent onto the shiny side of the patch and on the sanded area around the puncture and spread it to ensure maximum contact.

- Leave the adhesive for a moment to dry before pressing the patch over the puncture. Hold firmly until the patch and tube are firmly stuck together, and then lightly inflate.
- Place one bead of the tyre into position inside the rim.
- Place the valve in the valve hole in the rim and then feed the tube into position inside the tyre casing. This is easier

if the tube is lightly inflated to give it some shape.

- Starting at the valve, fit the loose side of the tyre back into the rim. Progressively feed the tyre bead into position inside the rim, working outward with both hands from the valve. When about 80% of the tyre is in position the resistance will prevent you getting any further. At this point you will need tyre levers. Be careful not to pinch the tube as you lever this last part of the tyre over the rim lip. This can cause another puncture before you even get the tyre back on!

- Pump the tyre to half the normal pressure and check that the tyre is correctly fitted to the rim. Inflate to full pressure and refit the wheel to your bike.

Simple enough, but it does take a little practice. Do that at home, before you go out on the bike – not at the roadside, all on your own, and some distance from civilization!

TOP *Replace the tube.*
CENTRE *Lever the tyre onto the rim.*
BOTTOM *Inflate the tyre.*

ACHIEVING TOP FORM

DO I HAVE TO TRAIN?

Well, if you want to get the best out of your cycling and enjoy the experience – then, yes, you have to train. However, it does not have to be an unpleasant task; it should be a part of the enjoyment of cycling. But first you need to understand what is meant by training.

Training is the road to fitness, which can be defined as the ability to carry out specific physical tasks, repeatedly, over a period, in an efficient manner.

In the context of any athletic pastime, simply carrying out the activity on a regular basis 'trains' the body to perform the activity. So it is with cycling. If you are riding regularly, then your body becomes more attuned to the activity and becomes 'trained' to carry it out. You become 'fit'.

Training for cycling-specific fitness can range from simply riding the bike at regular intervals for increasingly longer distances, to specialist forms of interval training designed to improve one or other of the rider's weak points.

The form of cycling you intend to do should determine your training routine. Someone whose intention is to tour on a bike designed to carry both rider and all his needs for an extended period of time will follow a different training regime to someone who is planning to ride cyclo-tourist events.

None of the work you do to improve your fitness should become drudgery. If you do not enjoy training, you will not derive benefit from it and will probably stop doing it.

TRAINING

GENERAL FITNESS

This refers to a level of fitness not specifically related to cycling. It is attained through any form of natural exercise. It matters not whether that exercise is derived from living a generally active life or from participating in some other sport, or even from the type of work carried out by the individual. It relates to the state of your body before you start any form of sport-specific training.

Any new rider with a reasonable level of basic fitness will be able to ride moderate distances without cycle-specific training. This will be accomplished without undue discomfort apart from cycling-specific areas of tenderness such as saddle soreness, a stiff neck or sore hands, due to the unfamiliarity of this kind of exercise.

This general level of fitness largely determines how much cycling-specific training will be required before the new rider starts to show improvement. And this will determine how soon the rider will start to derive greater enjoyment from cycling.

Someone who has played ball games regularly, or done athletics, for example, is likely to experience greater improvement over the first few months of cycling than a person who has led a sedentary life. Given the necessary perseverance, the sedentary person should be able to reach the same levels of cycling fitness as someone with a sporting background; it will just take longer.

RIDING THE BIKE

Riding your bike regularly is a fundamental component of any training programme, whether it is the basic training described in this chapter as LSD (*see p84*) or the more specialized training described further on in the chapter.

LEFT *A newcomer to cycling, who has achieved a reasonable level of basic fitness through other activities, will be able to ride moderate distances without discomfort.*
OPPOSITE *Riding your bike regularly is the most important component of your training programme, whether you are training for a race, time trials or a cycle touring holiday.*

REST

It has been said that it is not the training that you do that makes you fit; it is the rest you take after training that does it. The body is very adaptable and is able to make gradual changes to suit changing circumstances. During training your exertions break down cells in the muscles; then, while resting, the body proceeds to repair the damaged cells. When this pattern of exertion and repair happens on a regular basis, at appropriate intervals then, on each occasion, the cells are rebuilt a little stronger than previously. The most obvious example of this is that of body builders who, by carrying out specific exercises on a regular basis, are able to increase the size of their muscles.

SLEEP

The best rest, of course, is a good night's sleep. This is an oft-ignored, but very important, component of training and many riders do not reach their full potential simply because they ignore this. Between seven and eight hours a night is the norm for an athlete, but because individuals are unique, this is a generalization. Each athlete has to decide what is personally required through experimentation. An additional line in the training diary might be 'Hours sleep'. Then you can experiment by increasing or reducing the amount of sleep and comparing how you feel on the rides the following day. Over time, you will learn a great deal about your sleep requirements.

WHEN NOT TO RIDE

There are times when it is best not to ride, even if it disrupts your ideal training programme. If you have a cold or flu, then training is of little benefit, and the time would be better spent at home in bed.

If you have had a bad night's sleep, for whatever reason, and are feeling tired and listless, rather go home and catch up on the lost sleep. Also, if you have been injured in a fall, you should lay off training for a while to give the body time to recover.

TRAINING DIARY

It is a easier to train effectively if you have a training plan devised and written down. This also serves as motivation, and a copy should be kept where you will see it every day. Having set a plan, even if it is as simple as setting yourself a goal-distance to ride each day or week, you also need to record what you have achieved. Recording your achievements is a reward in itself and spurs you on to greater self-discipline when enthusiasm starts to flag.

Whatever your cycling aspirations, a record of the amount and intensity of the training

BELOW *The more enjoyable the training programme, the more likely you are to stick to it. Companionship usually helps.*

you do on a day-to-day basis collects data which can be used in the design of future training programmes.

Once you have been riding for a while and collected sufficient information in your training diary you will often identify programmes that failed or succeeded. This enables you to decide on the format of future training schedules with some factual reference to guide your decisions.

An example of the sort of information that should be kept on a regular basis is shown on page 84.

You should also record details of any organized or competitive event you might have ridden. A weekly

THERE ARE TIMES WHEN IT IS BEST NOT TO RIDE: IF YOU HAVE A COLD OR FLU; HAVE HAD LITTLE SLEEP; ARE RECOVERING FROM AN INJURY. THEN REST WILL BE OF MORE BENEFIT.

Date: 30/03/2004
Weather: Fine & sunny
Resting Pulse: 50
Ride route: Club house –
Castle Road – Main Street –
High Hill – home
Distance: 50km
Time: 1hr 22min
Intensity: Moderate
Group/Solo: Solo
Notes: Felt good apart
from High Hill.
Had to drop to 23 on the steep
bit instead of 21.
Felt fine on the rolling part.

summary should give the total distance covered, and also the total time spent on the bike.

Other information that could be recorded on a less frequent basis, say once a month, might be a record of weight and blood pressure.

The diary should also contain the measurements for the adjustments described in Chapter 4, in case you ever need to replicate the position on your bike (*see p51*).

BASIC OR LSD TRAINING

Basic (foundation) training is the formative work needed to start any athletic activity and is generally specific to the

ABOVE Sample page of a training diary.

activity. For cycling, it comprises regular rides done at a steady pace over gradually increasing distances. This is sometimes called LSD (Long Steady Distance) training.

By continuing to ride on a regular basis, usually several times a week, a cyclist will over time gradually train the body to perform the task better. Riding will become easier and more enjoyable. Greater distances will be covered with less fatigue and the horizons will be extended.

Generally, the beginner would join a club and partake in club riding activities, or go out on a regular basis with a group that cycles together frequently. This social riding helps to form a routine on which some form of training programme can be based later. The importance of this kind of group riding is that it gradually improves the rider's level of cycling-specific fitness and teaches skills that are not necessarily learned by riding alone. However, of necessity, most riders will spend much of their cycling time riding alone.

While LSD training is essential, if it is the only type of training you do, you will reach

a plateau beyond which you cannot improve with increased training. You will not go faster or further or climb hills better.

If you want to improve your time for a Century or finish in a better position in a cyclo-sportif, you'll need to train to ride faster, over longer distances, over more mountainous terrain. Your training will have to become more specialized as soon as you reach a level beyond which no discernible improvement can be made.

ADVANCED TRAINING METHODS

The human machine can only produce relatively low power. However, it can produce that power steadily for hours on end. If you increase the power output – to climb a hill faster, to close a gap between yourself and the group ahead, or simply to stay in the group – this increased output can only be sustained for a short time; sometimes for less than a minute.

To increase the level of power you can call on in short bursts or to extend the time for which the increased power is available, it is necessary to do more than just ride your bike.

Once you go beyond the basic training of regular LSD rides and move into more

BELOW Group riding is an enjoyable way of gradually improving a rider's cycling-specific fitness.

specialized forms of training, there is one principle you can apply immediately: alternate your training sessions. Most forms of specialized training are more strenuous than just riding the bike. You should alternate easy and hard training sessions on consecutive days, and break each week's training with either a rest day or an easy session (always on the day before an event for which you've entered), or any particularly strenuous ride that you have planned.

FARTLEK

Fartlek is a Swedish word that means speed-play. This form of training was devised by cross-country athletes 40 or 50 years ago, but is equally effective today. Applied to cycling, it is similar to interval training (*see p89*), but whereas true interval training is formalized, fartlek is not. It is best done in a group, but can be done by a single rider.

This session should take place over a distance that, depending on your level of fitness, would be a medium distance ride. It requires the ride to be done with no formal plan, at a variety of different speeds and over a variety of terrain, so that the intensity of the work being done is constantly changing.

Doing this in a group, with different members of the group dictating the pace at different times, it trains the body

RIGHT *Fartlek trains the body to react to the variations in pace that often occur in competitive riding.*

PULSE RATE

Ideally, interval training should be done based on the rider's pulse rate. Using a heart-rate monitor, the rest periods can be measured to allow the pulse rate to drop down to 60–70% of a predetermined maximum, while the high intensity work period should push the pulse rate into the 'training zone' – your 'target heart rate' calculated from your resting heart rate and age.

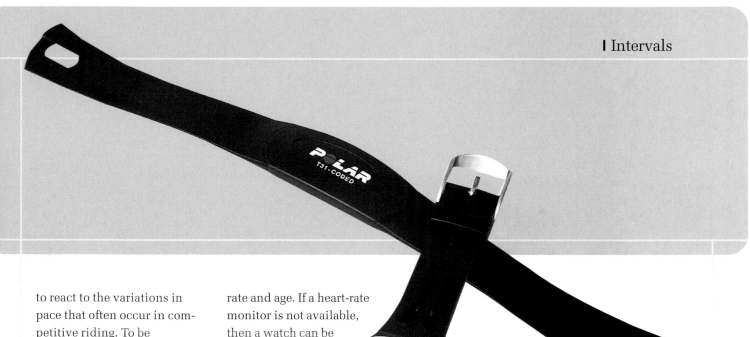

to react to the variations in pace that often occur in competitive riding. To be effective, a fartlek session should be tough and very demanding. It is for the rider who is serious about improving his performance in the more competitive rides.

INTERVALS

Interval training uses formal patterns of fast and slow riding. Broadly, short periods of high intensity work are alternated with periods of on-the-bike rest. It works on the training principle of progressive overload. This system can be used to develop either speed, stamina or strength in a very short time. The cardiovascular system derives high levels of benefit from this type of training.

Ideally, interval training should be done based on the rider's pulse rate. Using a heart-rate monitor, the rest periods can be measured to allow the pulse rate to drop down to 60–70% of a predetermined maximum, while the high intensity work period should push the pulse rate into the 'training zone' – your 'target heart rate' calculated from your resting heart rate and age. If a heart-rate monitor is not available, then a watch can be used and the intervals done on a time basis. For example, a 45-second work period alternated with a 1-minute rest period could be monitored with the use of an ordinary watch fixed to the handlebars, in easy view of the rider.

The timing of the work and rest periods determines the effect that this training will have on the body. If the work intervals are short (say 30 to 40 seconds) and very intense, while the rest periods are longer (say 1 to 1½ minutes), then this training session will achieve improvements in speed. A sprinter might use this type of session almost exclusively.

Conversely, if the work periods are longer (say 2 to 4 minutes) and done at lesser intensity, followed by rest periods not exceeding 30 seconds, this training session will improve stamina and endurance.

A third form of interval training would be for the work and rest periods to be equal (say one minute each), alternating a light gear (spinning the pedals) with a heavy gear. This will improve muscular strength.

These descriptions are of necessity brief in outline as the requirements of each rider are different and the intervals must be tailored to suit individual need.

Interval training is very economical in terms of the time needed to reach high levels of fitness, but it is very demanding (if done correctly) and cannot be said to be enjoyable.

ABOVE *Heart-rate monitors consist of two components, one worn around the chest, and the other around the wrist (or sometimes the handlebars).*

TRAINING TO CLIMB

Climbing is a pure strength exercise. It depends on a good power-to-weight ratio, which is why so many good climbers are small riders. However, climbing is also greatly assisted by the correct technique, and self-knowledge.

The only successful way of training to climb, is to practise regularly on steep gradients. Initially, simply including one reasonable climb in your training ride on two days of the week will suffice. As your general fitness improves so you should increase the number of rides that include a significant climb, and seek out climbs that are slightly steeper than the ones to which you are accustomed.

Once you have reached a level of fitness that cannot be improved with regular LSD rides, you will need to do more specialized training for climbing, too. If you have a long climb (10 minutes or more of climbing) within training reach of home, you can do short intervals on the climb. This may involve climbing at 100% effort for as little as 100m (330ft), followed by an interval of slower, less pressured climbing until your breathing and pulse have returned to an acceptable level. This works particularly well in a group if all riders have similar motivation.

Try training in a group

LEFT Manuel Beltran of Spain leads the main group up the Col de la Ramaz category one climb, followed by eventual Tour de France winner Lance Armstrong (left), during stage seven – from Lyon to Morzine-Avoriaz.

ABOVE Spinning is gym-based training, similar to aerobics, on a specialized stationary bicycle.

where some of the riders are a little better than you on the climbs and concentrate on staying with one of the stronger riders for as long as possible. At first you may not be able to last more than a few paces, but with regular practice you will find that you are able to remain with the stronger rider for longer and longer periods.

Another training method for climbing is to find a shorter climb and do a session of riding to the top and back to the bottom repetitively. The climbs should be done at 90% effort and the downhill return just freewheeling.

Some riders are natural climbers regardless of the training they do, but others will need to perfect their technique.

SPINNING

Spinning is gym-based training, similar to aerobics, using a specialized stationary bicycle. This is very useful for anyone who cannot get out on the road due to the weather, working hours, or other constraints. It is better than riding in the rain, and safer than riding in the dark with lights on, but it is not a substitute for riding the bike on a real road.

What spinning does very well is introduce riders to interval training, because much of a typical session comprises some form of interval training.

STRETCHING

Cycling is an activity that involves the muscles of the leg, thigh and ankle in a limited, repetitive turning motion. While cycling has many health benefits, this repetitive turning motion can have negative effects, which can be reduced by stretching.

The muscles used in turning the pedals are never able to fully extend or contract. If your position on the bike is set correctly so that you get the best performance from the effort that you expend, then the leg never straightens completely, nor is it permitted to bend as far as it might. As a result, while these muscles strengthen, they are also inclined to shorten due to the restricted movement. This, in turn, can lead to hamstring and knee injuries or result in lower back pain.

Long periods of cycling can result in a gradual loss of muscle elasticity and a reduction in the flexibility of the joints. A regular routine of stretching can help muscles and joints retain their suppleness and their full range of movement. Such a stretching routine can also reduce post-training muscle soreness.

The chart below shows some examples of stretching exercises recommended for cyclists.

LEFT *This is a good stretch for the quadriceps.*

A GLUTEUS MAXIMUS	G GROIN MUSCLES AND ADDUCTOR MUSCLES
B QUADRICEPS MUSCLE GROUP	H GROIN MUSCLES AND ADDUCTOR MUSCLES
C HAMSTRING MUSCLE GROUP AND SOLEUS	I NECK, BACK AND ABDOMINAL MUSCLES
D DELTOIDS OR SHOULDER AND ERECTOR SPINAL MUSCLES	J GLUTEAL MUSCLES
	K GLUTEAL MUSCLES
E HIP FLEXORS AND GROIN MUSCLES	L HAMSTRING MUSCLE GROUP AND BACK MUSCLES
F PECTORALS MUSCLES, THE GLUTEUS MAXIMUS AND THE OBLIQUE ABDOMINAL MUSCLES	M HAMSTRING MUSCLE GROUP AND CALF MUSCLES

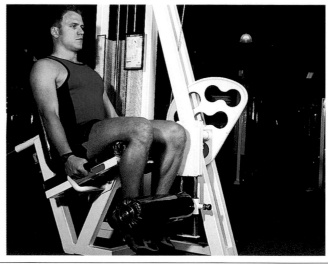

ABOVE Machine
leg extension.
RIGHT Seated machine
calf raise.

GYM WORK

Working out in a gym, either using weights or the various resistance machines, can be beneficial to a rider who is trying to increase strength, particularly if it is used to correct a particular weakness. If, however, you have limited training time, you will probably find that time spent riding your bike is of greater benefit.

In latitudes with very cold, dark winters, there is a period during the year when going out on the bike is unpleasant or simply not possible. That is when alternative methods of training, which can be done successfully indoors, are useful for maintaining your fitness.

If you have weaknesses that can be improved by strength training, then winter is a good time to train with weights, because you probably won't be

sacrificing time on the bike to do so. However, for effective weight training and to avoid injury, you need an instructor who will assist you in choosing the right exercises, and doing them correctly, so that you are most likely to achieve your aims.

For strength you need to use heavy weights and do fewer repetitions than you would if using weights for the purpose of achieving general fitness. Avoid injury by increasing loads in small increments.

You can also use weight training to achieve or maintain a level of general fitness by using lighter weights and performing more repetitions than you would for strength training exercises.

You have to remember that weight training for strength may also add bulk. This is fine for someone who is training for sprinting on the

velodrome, but not so good for a rider aiming to strengthen legs and back to be able to climb better.

Remember that training must be sport specific. While other training methods can help to improve deficiencies, the fact is that pushing weights to get fit will get you fit to push weights – not to ride a bike.

If the intention is to use the gym to replace cycling during the cold and damp period of winter, then the most effective would be a 1–1½ hour routine on two to three nights of the week and some other physical activity on another two nights. The weight training should be with light weights and many repetitions.

For those fortunate enough to live in a climate with good weather most of the year: why labour in a gym if you can be out there riding your bicycle?

TOP Prone leg curl.
ABOVE Seated leg press.

⠿ *DIET*

THE BODY'S USE OF FOODS

When doing regular exercise, nutrition will have a bearing on how much you enjoy what you are doing, and how much the exercise will develop your body.

THIS PAGE Nuts, fish and, in small quantities, red meat, are good sources of protein, which contains the basic building blocks for repairing and renewing body cells. This is essential for developing power in the legs.

There are reams of literature available on nutrition for athletes of all types and all levels of ability, but a basic understanding of how the body uses food as fuel will go a long way toward making the cycling experience more productive.

The food we eat is made up of protein, fats and carbohydrates.

PROTEIN

Protein is not a good source of energy. Its purpose is to repair cells injured by exertion. Proteins contain the building blocks used to repair and renew body cells (*see p82*).

The normal daily protein requirement of 1.5–2 grams of protein per kilogram of body mass (0.0015–0.002% of body mass) is easily met by a diet sufficient to replenish the energy used during the day.

Protein contains amino acids, which, besides building cells and repairing tissue, also form antibodies to combat invading bacteria and viruses. These amino acids are absorbed from the protein during digestion and distributed to cells throughout the body by means of the circulatory system, and used to rebuild damaged cells. In the process of protein being broken down by digestion, 20 known amino acids are released. Eight of these are essential, because the body does not produce them itself, whereas it can produce the remainder with the correct nutrition.

The body does not store protein. Cell repair during the recovery period following any form of exercise is carried out by the protein ingested from the meal eaten afterward.

Any small amounts of surplus protein will then be converted into fats or carbohydrates.

FATS

In a normal Western diet, fats supply 20% to 40% of the daily calorie requirement. About 95% of dietary fat consists of triglycerides (fats composed of a glycerol molecule and three fatty acid molecules). They are used primarily as a source of energy. The other 5% of fat consists of cholesterol and phospholipids, essential building blocks for cell growth. Fats are a prime energy source for the endurance athlete – particularly cyclists covering long distances.

Any excess fats are stored in fat cells in the body.

CARBOHYDRATES

Simple carbohydrates are found in foods such as fruit, some vegetables, honey and milk, which are considered healthy and nutritious, as well as in those refined sugars, considered less nutritious, sweets and cakes.

Complex carbohydrates occur in foods such as potatoes, pasta and other grain products. They should provide more than 60% of the calories needed by an active person.

Simple carbohydrates are absorbed into the blood during digestion and energy is available 30 minutes after ingestion. Complex carbohydrates take longer to become available. Unused energy is stored as glycogen in the liver and in the cells of the muscles. This store of energy remains available for immediate requirements.

While exercising, whether training or on long rides, the body first uses muscle glycogen for its energy supply and then draws on the glycogen reserves in the liver.

The body's stores of glycogen are limited to about 100 minutes of aerobic activity. After 1½ to 2 hours of exercise, when these glycogen reserves are depleted, the body starts using fat reserves unless there is glucose circulating in the bloodstream from food eaten during the ride.

Most of the time your riding is done aerobically – there is more than enough oxygen present in the body cells to metabolize glycogen. When the level of effort becomes anaerobic (energy requirement outstrips the cardiovascular system's ability to provide oxygen), then the energy obtained from glycogen is drastically reduced. This is part of the reason why such extreme effort can only be sustained for very short periods of time.

BASIC NUTRITION FOR SPORT

To find the best diet for you, you have to explore different foods, give them a trial period and, if they do not work for you, try something else. You need to keep an open mind, even when you've chanced upon your optimum diet, because your body is changing all the time, and what works fine today might not do the trick in a year's time. You have to be flexible.

You also need some knowledge of what typical energy requirements are.

THIS PAGE Fruit and vegetables should make up the bulk of your diet.

Fat reserves are virtually unlimited – a typical 70kg (150 lb) male probably has around 130,000–140,000 calories available. However, immediate requirements are met by glycogen reserves stored in muscle tissue and in the liver, but those reserves are limited to 1500–2000 calories.

The approximate daily energy requirements for a typical sedentary 70kg (150 lb) adult male is estimated to be 2000–2200 cal/day. A touring cyclist covering 80 to 100km/day (50–60 miles/day) at a moderate pace requires over 5000 cal/day. A professional racing cyclist's requirements can exceed 8000 cal/day.

The maximum energy consumption of a trained athlete is about 1000 calories per hour.

A 40km (25-mile) ride done at close to maximum pace would take roughly one hour and require some 1000 calories. The same distance at a leisurely pace would use somewhat less energy.

Based on the advice of nutritionists an ideal diet for a fit cyclist should consist of 60–70% carbohydrate, 10–15% protein and 20–30% fat.

The recommended intake for an athlete is 10 grams of carbohydrate for every kilogram (2.2 lb) of body weight per day. Therefore, an athletic 70kg (154 lb) male would require a minimum 700 grams of carbohydrate per day to produce 2800 calories which, if this represents 60–70% of his diet, gives him a total intake of 4000 to 4500 calories per day.

Now examine what you eat and see how close you are to the ideal.

Some typical food components are given in the following chart.

FATS

POULTRY, EGGS

LEGUMES

FISH

NUTS, SEEDS, OLIVE OIL

LOW-FAT DAIRY

WHOLE GRAINS AND CEREALS

FRUIT AND VEGETABLES

WATER

REDUCE INTAKE OF

White bread, sweets,
sugar, cakes, pastries,
alcohol

AVOID WHEN POSSIBLE

Artificial sweeteners
Additives & preservatives
Smoked & processed foods
Flavour enhancers

FOOD CHART

Keep a record of what you eat over a week or so and rectify any imbalances. Perhaps you should include more of one group or another, or you may have forgotten one group altogether. Personal preferences are a guide to what your body requires, but it is important to be flexible. Explore different foods, give them a trial period. If they do not work for you, try something else.

EATING & DRINKING ON THE MOVE

On any ride that will last more than 1–1½ hours, you should carry food with you and eat small amounts regularly throughout the ride to ensure that you replace the energy you are using up. If you do not eat there is a risk that you will experience what is usually termed 'the bonk,' or more colourfully 'hitting the wall'. More correctly, it is a glycogen deficit. You will suddenly feel very weak, possibly light-headed and unable to turn the pedals to any good effect. You have run out of fuel.

The fuel is glycogen, which the body produces from the food you eat. The body carries roughly 1½ hour's worth of glycogen, so a one-hour ride can be done comfortably without replenishment. Longer than that depends on the individual (the heavier you are the more fuel you burn); and on the intensity of the ride (the harder you ride the more fuel you will use).

Cycling jerseys have pockets at the back where it is easy to get to the contents. While these are great for carrying your wallet, a rain jacket and a spare tube, they are actually intended for carrying the food you need for the ride. There are many choices and you will have to experiment with different things to find what works best for you.

Whatever provisions you carry, that food is what your body will convert into the glycogen it requires to fuel your engine. Energy bars are very effective, designed for just this purpose, but equally effective are simple things like a banana or even small sandwiches.

One rider might find, for example, that fruit cake is the ideal food, while another cannot eat it at any cost. Try things that appeal to you, and try things that your training companions use.

Whatever you use it must be something that can be stored easily in the pockets of the cycling jersey; is palatable to you; and will provide the body with carbohydrates that can quickly and easily be converted into glycogen.

Drinking while on the move is more important than eating. It is essential to keep hydrated. During the ride, you lose copious amounts of body fluid through perspiration. With that fluid loss, there is also a significant loss of minerals.

You should be drinking at regular intervals throughout the ride. Not only do you need water to keep the

ABOVE Pre-packaged fuel, free of preservatives, colourants or flavourants!

RIGHT Cycling jerseys have pockets at the back where it is easy to reach the contents.

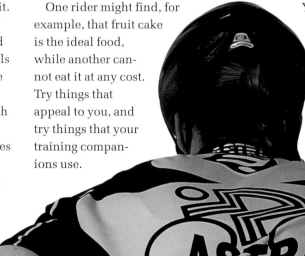

RECOVERY EATING

Immediately after exercise, there is a period of about one hour during which you should eat to recover. During this short period after riding, the muscles absorb nutrients more efficiently and need protein to rebuild damaged cells. Also, this is when the glycogen reserves in the muscles, which you have depleted on the ride, are replaced most efficiently. You should not eat a heavy meal, but concentrate on carbohydrate snacks or drinks.

DOS AND DON'TS

• Do drink regularly while riding.
• Don't go out on a ride without at least one bottle of fluid to drink.
• Do eat regularly on any ride of over 1½ hours.
• Don't go out without food in your pockets, even on a short ride.
• Do eat small amounts of food regularly, even when off the bike.
• Don't eat big meals.
• Do eat to recover within an hour after the ride.

LEFT *It is important to drink regularly while riding – dehydration impairs performance and can be dangerous.*

BELOW *Fruit not only is a good source of energy, but is free of additives, packed with vitamins and usually convenient to eat while riding.*

body hydrated, but also because it helps the body absorb the necessary minerals in the food you eat. While plain water is fine in the drinking bottle, it is more efficient for the water to be carrying some form of carbohydrate so that, as you drink, so you replenish some of the minerals lost through sweat as well as carbohydrates used during the ride.

If you have drunk well in the hour before the ride, you should be able to ride about 2–2½ hours on the contents of a 500ml (1pt) drinking bottle. If you plan to ride longer than that, then a 750ml (1½pt) bottle, or two cages and two 500ml (1pt) bottles would be better; alternatively, plan a stop for refreshment at about half distance. It is important not to run dry.

ABOVE *Descents take practice and self-control. Here Tyler Hamilton descends the Col de Galibier during stage eight, from Sallanches to L'Alpe d'Huez, of the Tour de France.*

OPPOSITE *Bunch riding in the Tour de France. Here Lance Armstrong leads the peloton through the French countryside during stage 17 between Dax and Bordeaux.*

RIDING TECHNIQUES

STARTING OFF

When you were a child, you simply leapt onto the bike and rode it without any thought other than where you were going. Generally, that was somewhere relatively local, and if by chance, you got a flat tyre, it really was not far to walk home.

A modern road bike makes journeys of several hours the norm. This requires a little more thought before you set off. Even a one-hour ride into the open countryside could take you 14–15km (9–10 miles) away from home – a long way to walk if you had even a simple breakdown.

When setting off on a ride it should become a habit to check a few essentials: that the tyres are properly inflated and that you have at least one spare tube, either in the saddlebag or in your pocket, along with a pair of tyre levers. Two spare tubes are better (the extra tube takes up little additional space). Otherwise, some patches and a tube of patching adhesive are good insurance against a second puncture.

If, on short rides, you prefer to dispense with the little saddlebag and simply carry what is necessary in your pocket, then take a spare tube folded up to the length of a tyre lever, and secured with the two levers, all held together with a rubber band. This makes a neat enough package to slip into your pocket.

Having checked the tyres and spare, you should just lift the bike and spin the wheels front and back to ensure that they are not touching the brake pads and are running true. Lastly, a quick dab on the brake levers to ensure that the brakes are actually stopping the wheel, before you swing your leg over the saddle, clip into the pedals and set off on another day's riding.

RIDING ALONE

Many riders go solo much of the time. While it is always better to ride in a group, or with a buddy, your daily routine probably dictates when a few precious hours can be spent on riding. Also, the difficulty of trying to arrange times convenient to a group of riders, who all have their own time constraints, means that during the working week it is often necessary to ride alone.

When riding alone you need to be extra alert. In a group there are several pairs of eyes to spot something that a solo rider would have missed. In traffic, a single rider is more difficult to see from a speeding motor vehicle, which makes the solo rider more vulnerable.

If your solo rides are intended as training to improve your fitness level, then you need to have a definite plan for your ride if you are to make good use of it. The different forms of training that you can use are covered in Chapter 6.

You will not gain as much if you ride aimlessly, because you are likely to ride more slowly than if you were training to a plan or with a group. On the other hand, very often the aimless rides are the enjoyable ones and the benefits are other than physical.

An ideal way of using the days when you have to ride solo anyway is to use the bike to commute to college or work. Often a little planning in terms of clothing and a

place to wash can pay huge dividends, both in your training, in the use of time otherwise lost in commuting by car, bus or train and, not least, there's a saving in cost.

THIS PAGE When riding with a buddy, you are more likely to stick to a training plan. Solo rides can become aimless unless you set a definite goal.

OPPOSITE Bunch riding is honed to a fine art by professional teams. Here a team sets the pace on the Col de Soudet during stage 16 of the Tour de France.

RIDING IN A GROUP

Whether the ride is serious training or just a casual ramble across the countryside, riding in a group has many benefits.

As racing cyclists prove continuously, a group will travel faster than a solo rider; or will travel at the same speed with far less effort. Aerodynamic principles permit the riders who are sheltered by others in the group to use less effort to maintain a speed that, alone, they could only maintain for a short time. Riders take turns being at the front of the group. After doing a short stint at the front setting the pace, they then move to the rear to benefit from the shelter provided by the others, while rested riders move to the front to do a period of harder work, before they, too, retire to the shelter of the group. This is variously termed 'pacing' or 'drafting'. The faster or harder the group is riding, the greater the benefit felt by all. However, the system is still beneficial at lower speeds.

The group as is far more visible to other traffic than a single rider and is less likely to be involved in an accident involving another vehicle. There is, of course, the risk in a group that two riders may collide, fall and bring others off as well.

One drawback with group riding is that legislation in some parts of the world

LEFT *The peloton rides through the French countryside between Troyes and Nevers.*

ABOVE *Ensure that your front wheel does not overlap the rear wheel of the rider in front of you.*

OPPOSITE *The peloton makes its way up the first climb outside Turin in Italy.*

BELOW *If you are at the front, you should set the pace at a speed that can be maintained by the weakest rider in the group.*

prohibits cyclists from riding side by side at any time, irrespective of the width of the road or the density of traffic. Experienced riders in your club or training group will know the laws and regulations in your area.

Some rules to follow when riding in a group are:

- Ensure that your front wheel does not overlap the rear wheel of the rider in front of you. This is to avoid your wheel being knocked by the one in front of you, if the rider were to swerve for any reason. This could cause you to fall and, in a bunch, bring other riders down too.
- Signal your intentions either by hand or voice if you are about to change position in the bunch. Any sudden move to left or right without warning could cause a rider behind you to swerve, resulting in a chain reaction throughout the bunch. This is often the reason for falls in a group.
- If you need to stop for any reason, make sure that the riders behind you are aware that you are about to do so.
- If you are at the front setting the pace, try to keep the speed at a level that can be maintained by the weakest rider in the group.
- The group should wait for a member who suffers a puncture. Don't leave the rider to replace a tube and then chase after the group to catch up.

INTO THE WIND

One of the great frustrations for newcomers to cycling is contending with the wind and the feeling that they are putting in huge amounts of effort without progressing at all.

If you live in an area where strong winds are prevalent for at least part of the year, then you will need to learn patience. You cannot fight the wind. If there is a strong headwind, all you can do is use a lower gear and try to keep a regular cadence of 80 to 90 pedal revolutions per minute. Riding in strong wind is a little like climbing a long hill – a strength exercise.

If you are part of a group, then sharing the workload, as described above, is important, because it will help to shelter you from at least some of the wind and enable you to keep a reasonable pace for the short period that you are at the front of the group.

In these conditions, it is best to make changes on a more regular basis, the riders at the front keeping their time there to a minimum. Care is needed when positioning yourself in the slipstream of the rider in front of you to get the best protection from the wind. In this instance it is more important than ever not to overlap wheels, because gusts can cause even the best riders to weave.

When toiling into a headwind, remind yourself that the wind is making you strong and that you will benefit from the work you're putting in under those conditions. Also, if you have planned your ride with foresight, you will have a tailwind all the way home!

AERODYNAMIC PRINCIPLES PERMIT THE RIDERS WHO ARE SHELTERED BY THE OTHERS IN THE GROUP TO USE LESS EFFORT TO MAINTAIN A SPEED THAT, ALONE, THEY COULD ONLY MAINTAIN FOR A SHORT TIME.

CLIMBING

Part of the technique of climbing is having and using the correct gear ratios. Another part is learning to pace yourself.

The correct gear ratio, like so many things in athletic endeavour, depends on the individual. For climbing, lower-than-normal gears are needed – that is to say, bigger sprockets at the rear and the smallest chainring at the front. The problem is to know what size sprockets to have on the wheel and which to use for any particular gradient.

Inexperienced riders are most likely to tackle a climb all out, without giving a thought to pacing themselves to the top. This forces the pulse rate to climb and blood pressure to rise. The rider becomes tense and burns energy at a higher rate than he would have done had he paced himself carefully. Generally, this tactic results in the rider being dropped on the climb, unable to breathe in sufficient oxygen to help fuel tiring muscles.

On any given gradient, out of a group of 10 experienced riders, two might be using a 25-tooth sprocket, four a 24-tooth, three a 23 and one a 21. So who is right? The rider on the 21 would probably be struggling to turn over too big a gear (a gear ratio too high for the conditions) and making the strength exercise harder than it need be. The riders on

LEFT The climb leading to the Col du Tourmalet between Bagnères-de-Bigorre and Luz-Ardiden. Jan Ulrich leads Lance Armstrong.

25-tooth sprockets are probably under-geared because they feel they do not have the strength, and will be struggling to turn the pedals over fast enough to stay with the group.

Of the rest on 23- or 24-tooth sprockets, some might be over-geared for their individual abilities while some might be on what is, for them, the ideal gear for that climb.

Only by trial and error can you find the perfect gear for any incline. The best way is to experiment on a local climb until you find the ratio that feels right for you on that gradient. You can then, wherever you go, mentally compare your local climb with any other climb and have a fairly good idea of what gear you will need.

Most good lightweight racing bikes will have a range of gears suitable for a wide range of terrain so that riders seldom have to change sprockets. However, there may be occasions when it is necessary. For example:

- if you were going on an extended tour with panniers and racks fitted to carry a substantially greater load than usual;
- riding a longer than normal cyclo-tourist event or randonneur where, in the latter stages, tired legs may not be able to turn over what, under normal circumstances, would be a moderate ratio;
- or an event with larger

climbs than you would normally tackle.

Any of these conditions would dictate changing the cluster of sprockets for one giving larger sprockets at the low end of the range of ratios. This would normally be a job for the cycle dealer. Remember, if the dealer is changing over the sprockets, get him to put a new chain on at the same time. Retain the sprockets and chain that came off your bike, so that you can get him to put them back when you return to normal rides again. Likewise, once you put your bike back to normal gears, retain the larger set, together with the chain you used on them so that they are available when needed in future.

None of this implies that a climb should be done in one gear. Often it is possible to climb the earlier slopes of the climb in a higher (or lower) gear than you would need near the top. Changing gears part way up the climb takes a bit of practice, but can often be the difference between topping the climb with the group, or grovelling in a little later!

On group rides, try to position yourself in the bunch so that you are at the side of, or on the wheel of, an experienced rider that you can 'shadow' up the climb, and learn by observation how to pace yourself. It is also an opportunity to

study the technique of a more experienced rider.

Another method is to reach the start of the climb at the front of the group and drift back in the bunch, as stronger riders start to pass you. You should aim to lose only the length of the group during the climb so that you breast the top of the climb last, but still in contact, having climbed at a slightly lower speed than the rest of the riders.

DESCENDING

For some, a steep mountain descent is an adrenaline rush; for others it is naked fear.

Dropping down a precipit-ous mountainside at over 80kph (50mph) holds certain risks. As with most of the risks that litter life, understanding the risk is a large step toward reducing it to size.

If the descent is relatively straight with good visibility of most of the roadway ahead, then the apparent risk is mini-mized in the minds of most people. Most of the fear of descending is the unknown beyond the next corner, for usually mountain descents have many twists and turns on the route to the valley below. Any one of these twists could hide some hazard beyond the line of sight.

Cyclists for whom plunging down a steep decline is all hot excitement are often tempted to cut the corners, to 'flatten

helps if you are making your descent at a controlled speed that is within your bike handling capabilities. Demon descents with the rider on the ragged edge of disaster may look great in films of the Tour de France, but unless you are actually in a competitive event where every second counts, it is not worth the risk.

BRAKING

While you may spend most of your riding time with your hands on the brake hoods, fingers resting on the top of the levers, there are times when 'down on the drops' (bottom bend of the handlebar) is the best place to be. When the wind is in your face, or you are hanging on in a fast-moving pack, or on a descent, where down on the drops provides the best bike control, you need to be feathering the brakes with one finger resting on the lever close to that little curl at the end. One finger's pressure on the lever is sufficient to drag speed off as fast as tyre adhesion will allow.

The correct position of the brake levers will make this one-finger feathering easier. If the levers are set up incorrectly on the bend of the handlebar, you will not be able to reach the lever comfortably. Adjust the position of the levers until you can reach them easily. If you have to move your hands from their position on the bars to reach

the levers, that little bit of extra time taken could be the difference between a safe dab of the brakes and a fall.

Tyre adhesion helps you stop safely. As soon as the tyre loses adhesion, braking ceases and you lose control. A sudden snatch at the brake levers usually has the effect of bringing both wheels to an abrupt halt, while momentum ensures that you and your bike continue, but no longer with any control. Learn to judge the maximum braking pressure, which is just before the tyres lose adhesion. Apply braking pressure gradually, using one or two fingers. This is normally sufficient even in panic situations.

When you approach a corner, the brakes should be applied just before you alter your line to enter the corner. Both levers should be applied with even pressure – not snatched at. By the time you are into the turn you should be off the brakes and accelerating out of the apex of the corner. That way you also carry your momentum through the corner, resulting in less effort having to be expended in accelerating back up to speed.

There is a belief that one should never use the front brake only. However, particularly when riding in a bunch, light feathering of the front brake only, provides the best control. Obviously, too much front brake could have

out' the curve of the bend by taking a straight line, even though it may take them over the centre line, which could be into the face of oncoming traffic. This practice simply adds to the risk and should not be tried when visibility across the corner is obstructed.

Descending takes practice and self-control. Much of the fear of what is round the next corner can be eliminated if your cornering technique is good and you are confident of your bike handling. It also

disastrous consequences – as disastrous as slamming on the back brake alone. However, it is not emergency stopping, or even stopping, that is being discussed here, but rather bike control. Feathering the front brake simply provides better control than trying to do the same thing using the rear brake. You are not applying the brake sufficiently hard to cause the wheel to stop and pitch you onto your head.

When you decelerate (whether by using front or rear brakes), the weight of machine and rider moves forward. With less weight on the rear wheel, it has less grip and you have less control over what it's doing. In an emergency stop it might even fish-tail because, once it loses traction, it can as well slide sideways as forward. So, when you practise panic stops, don't shy away from using the front brake – learn to use both brakes effectively, keeping in mind that the rear wheel will lose traction, and thus effectiveness, as you decelerate.

Remember, the brakes could be your best friend. Be gentle with them.

CORNERING

Bicycles are not steered like a motor vehicle. It is not necessary to turn the handlebars to the right in order to turn right. Even at low speeds bicycles turn corners when the rider leans the machine into the corner.

By honing your cornering skills you can save a little time by getting through corners faster. It will also enable you to experience exhilaration, instead of fear, on a swift drop down a winding mountain pass, safe in the knowledge that your cornering skills are up to the task.

When you lean the bike into a corner, the outside leg should be straight, and you should be placing your weight on this outside pedal as you go through the corner, to keep the body balanced over the bike. The inside foot should be up at the top of the pedal's turning circle with the knee bent and pointing into the turn. As you lean the bike, apply slight pressure on the handlebar on the side to which you are

turning. This causes the front wheel to turn very slightly in the opposite direction to that in which you are turning. If you have ever ridden a motorcycle you will probably already be aware of this phenomenon.

Concentrate on applying pressure on the outer pedal, to keep your weight balanced across the bike. Remember to sit firmly on the saddle and have the hands down on the drops, fingers positioned lightly on the brake levers.

As you approach a corner, provided that traffic conditions allow, move to the outside edge of the lane you are in (NOT across the centre line) and aim across toward the apex of the corner. The purpose is to ride as straight a line as possible through the corner. This allows you to go through the corner faster than you would if you hugged the inside edge of the road.

Be aware of road conditions. On wet roads, or on loose surfaces such as gravel or sand, you need to be more

ABOVE *Cornering during a high-speed descent requires nerve and skill, as demonstrated by this bunch on a hill between Gap and Marseille.*

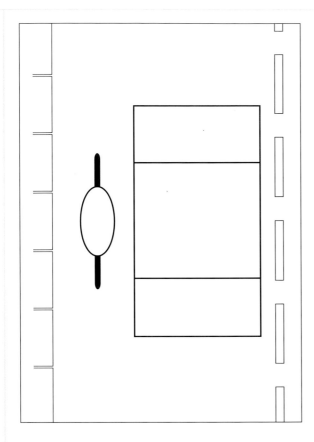

ABOVE *The safest place is about 1m (3ft) out from the kerb. This gives you room to manoeuvre when a long vehicle passes you and starts to move over to the nearside.*

conservative in how far you lean the bike. Losing the bike in a turn is painful as well as embarrassing. Cornering is a skill requiring practice.

IN TRAFFIC

Riding in traffic varies from city to city and from one part of the globe to another. The greatest difference is probably that in different parts of the world the rule of the road may be either to 'keep right' or 'keep left', depending on whether you're in mainland Europe and the Americas, or in the UK and its former dominions. Therefore, for the purpose of this

section on riding in traffic I will use the term 'nearside' for that side of the road where you ride in the same direction as the traffic and 'offside' for the opposite side of the road, where you face on-coming traffic. Quaint, but it works.

City traffic can be dangerous for cyclists, but relatively safe if you are aware of the dangers and ride defensively. Some of the risks inherent in riding in any urban location are:

• Not being seen by motorists.
• Not being given enough space by motorists passing at speed.
• Having long vehicles move over before it is safe to do so.
• Pedestrians.
• Roadside 'furniture' such as road signs and refuse bins.
• Junctions.

One would think that a fully grown person on a bicycle would be visible in broad daylight, but a motorist fighting city traffic, in a hurry, late for an appointment, with a thousand distractions all around, can fail to see a cyclist. It happens.

A good defence is to wear bright, colourful clothing. Remember that you are competing for the motorist's attention with many other distractions in the muddle and bustle of city life. To survive you need to stand out. Wear sober black, grey or brown and the next thing you hear might be a motorist claiming: 'I didn't see the cyclist.'

Fluorescent cross-belts worn over normal clothing are also highly visible, particularly in adverse weather or when visibility is poor.

Traffic regulations worldwide frequently stipulate that bicycles sharing the roadway with other vehicular traffic should keep well to the nearside of the carriageway (all the lanes moving in the same direction). As a first step in defensive riding, treat this stipulation with some caution. On a section of city street not lined with parked cars, the safest place for you to be is about 1m (3ft) out from the kerb. This gives you room to manoeuvre when a long vehicle passes you and starts to move over to the nearside. It also makes you more visible to motorists approaching from behind.

Where cars are parked all along the kerb, treat the line of cars as the kerb and keep 1m (3ft) out from them. Where cars are only parked intermittently down the nearside of the roadway, keep a straight line. Don't weave in and out of the empty parking spaces. Each time you weave out into the carriageway to clear a parked car you run the risk of appearing suddenly in the line of travel of a motorist who hadn't seen you.

When you approach an intersection where you intend going straight, be sure that the motorist coming up behind you is aware of your intention. The driver might plan on turning at this junction and decide to pass and turn across your line of travel, with potentially disastrous results. A hand signal, pointing toward the offside should warn any motorist intending to turn in front of you.

Probably the situation with the greatest potential for an accident is when you want to turn at a junction across a lane of oncoming traffic. Indicate your intention before you make any effort to change direction. At the same time glance over your shoulder to assess where approaching cars are and when it is safe to cross. Then move smartly to the other side of the carriageway. Once safely there, take account of oncoming traffic, whose path you are going to cross, to complete your turn. Keep indicating so that drivers behind you, turning in the same direction, and drivers approaching you from the opposite direction are aware of your intention to turn.

Finally, be conscious of your surroundings when you are riding in traffic. Watch for potential hazards ahead of you, for example – don't wait until you are almost on top of a manhole cover before you swerve to avoid it. You should gradually alter your line so that you pass round any obstruction without violent change of direction. Watch out for pedestrians trying to cross the road, particularly where there are parked cars obstructing the view ahead.

Make this your mantra: See – Be Seen – Be Alert.

SIGN LANGUAGE

Signal your intentions. This is the single most valuable safety precaution. This applies equally to city commuting, where you are sharing the road with motorized commuters, as to a ride through the countryside with a group of like-minded cyclists.

If you have the opportunity to ride with a group in another country you will find that many of the hand signals they use differ from what you are used to in your country. Usually the signs are self-evident, for example, a hand flapped up and down at hip height usually means a warning to slow down, while directional signals are normally a hand pointing in the direction that the rider plans to move. Whatever the differences, the golden rule remains – signal your intentions.

In a group, of course, you can call out your intentions because everyone in the group is usually within hearing range; not so, unfortunately, when indicating to other traffic. The driver of the motor vehicle bearing down on you as you start to turn across his path, cannot hear anything you might call out, but he is

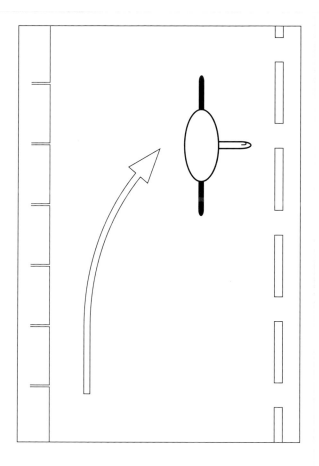

likely to see a hand indicating the direction in which you intend to turn.

If you are new to cycling, or have moved to another country, get a copy of the local Highway Code. Most Highway Codes around the world apply similar rules to users of the public highway, but there will be variations. Remember that almost without exception the Highway Code will have been written with motorists in mind and there will be little relating specifically to cyclists. If that is the case, look up what they recommend for motorcyclists.

ABOVE When turning at a junction across a lane of oncoming traffic, indicate your intention, glance over your shoulder to assess where approaching cars are, then move smartly to the other side of the carriageway. Once safely there, take account of oncoming traffic, whose path you are going to cross, to complete your turn.

WET WEATHER

Wet weather adds a new dimension to cycling – often a wet, uncomfortable one – but also with its own hazards and corresponding techniques to help you cope.

There are two things to remember when the rain starts: your tyres' grip on the road surface is much reduced and your brake pads, when wet, will not slow down your progress as much as in dry weather.

What this means is that if you were to approach a corner at the same speed as you would in the dry, you will almost certainly fall off. Your brakes will not slow you down soon enough and with reduced grip on the road surface as you bank into the bend, the tyres will break away and down you will come. It is a painful lesson that many cyclists learn by practical experience.

The answer to this little problem has two parts: adapt your braking and cornering techniques. Firstly, once it starts raining, keep some light pressure on the brake levers. The pads rubbing against the wheel rims wipe away the water so that, when you need the brakes, there is less of a delay before the pads bite and reduce your speed. Secondly, when cornering, try to keep the bike more upright than you would in the dry, by leaning your body more into the turn than the bicycle itself.

In heavy rain, visibility is reduced for rider and motorist alike. However, the cyclist's vision is further reduced by stinging raindrops and water running into the eyes. Glasses with clear or yellow lenses provide the best visibility in heavy rain; but even normal sunglasses will, in some conditions, provide better visibility than riding into rain with nothing to protect your eyes.

When riding in company, try not to ride directly behind the rider in front of you, even if the wind is coming from straight in front and this position offers the best shelter. The reason for avoiding this is that the front rider's back wheel will be throwing up water and grit (even if the bike is fitted with mudguards) which, apart from the fact that you will be getting even wetter, can cause you to collide – if your stopping distance is less than that of the front rider. If you are riding to one side and are not able to slow as quickly as the front rider you are usually able to go down the side rather than directly into the back wheel.

Make sure that your rain jacket or cape is a bright yellow or orange as rain reduces visibility. The golden rule in the wet is: caution.

ABOVE *Wet weather glasses protect your eyes so that you don't have to reduce your vision by ducking and squinting against raindrops and splatter.*

OPPOSITE *Wet weather reduces your tyres' grip and the efficiency of brake pads.*

BELOW *Bright raingear makes you visible to road traffic in rainy conditions.*

8

SAFETY & PROTECTION

HELMETS, MITTS AND UNDERSHIRTS

Like almost everything else we do, cycling is potentially dangerous. These activities can be relatively harmless if we are aware of the risks and take the appropriate precautions. Cycling requires a few precautions too, no matter how far we plan on riding. Since riding a bicycle involves balancing on two wheels, there is always the risk of a fall. Most falls are of minor consequence but they can involve injury.

The most vulnerable part of the anatomy is the head. Modern bicycle helmets are believed to prevent some 85% of head injuries in cycling accidents. They absorb the energy of a violent blow. Most helmets achieve this with expanded polystyrene (EPS) as used in the packaging industry. The helmet is moulded in

this soft material and then covered with an outer skin of a harder plastic. The expanded polystyrene absorbs the force of any blow to the head in the event of a fall, while the harder outer shell permits the helmet to skid across the road surface reducing the risk of snagging and jerking the neck while the rider is sliding out of control. The expanded polystyrene does not recover. Once crushed it stays crushed and the helmet needs to be replaced. Expensive? Yes, but cheaper than head injuries.

Helmets are made to a number of similar standards. The most trusted are SNELL, ANSI, and BS (UK). In each case, the fact that the helmet complies with the relevant standard will be detailed on a label inside. That is the kind you should buy. Never ride without one.

The helmet should fit snugly on the head without being too tight. The fit can be improved by adjusting the straps. This takes a bit of trial and error. Finding the right adjustment so that the buckles do not dig into your chin will add to the comfort.

Most helmets come with adjustable pads inside the helmet that can be moved about to achieve a perfect fit. When the helmet is correctly adjusted it should not be perched on the back of the head. The front edge of the helmet should be at a point near the centre of your forehead, a couple of centimetres above the eyebrows.

ABOVE *The lightweight modern helmet is designed with ventilation slots for coolness.*
BELOW *Helmet cut-away*

In some countries, the wearing of a helmet is obligatory when cycling on a public road, and most organized events make it a condition of entry. Even when there is free choice, there can be no reasonable argument for taking the risk of riding without a helmet.

There are other items of clothing that can reduce the risk or at least the extent of injuries in the event of a fall. A simple precaution is to wear at least two layers of clothing – yes, even on a hot day. If, in the event of a fall, you have only one layer of clothing, it sticks to your body and the road surface eats through it as you slide – and then eats into your skin. Road rash, as this is sometimes called, is uncomfortable at the least. When you wear two layers, the outer layer slides against the undergarment, acting almost like a lubricant,

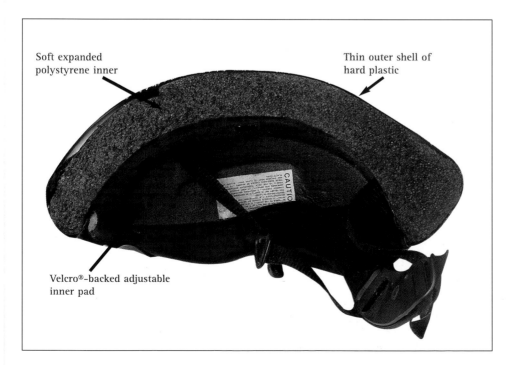

Soft expanded polystyrene inner

Thin outer shell of hard plastic

Velcro®-backed adjustable inner pad

HELMET POSITION

Most helmets also come with adjustable pads inside the helmet and moving these about often brings about a perfect fit. When the helmet is correctly adjusted it should not be perched on the back of the head. The front edge of the helmet should be at a point near the centre of your forehead, a couple of centimetres above the eyebrows.

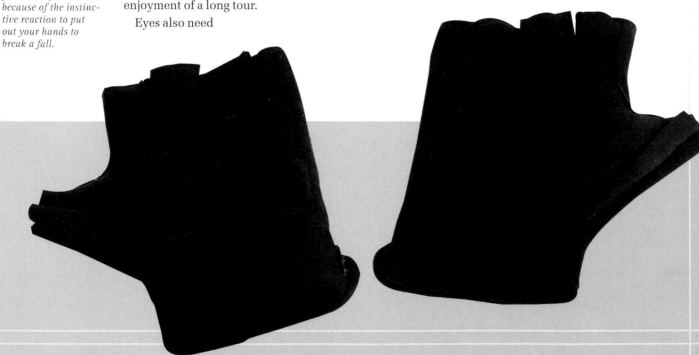

ABOVE *Eyes need protection against sun, wind and grit. Vision impaired even momentarily by tearing, can lead to disaster.*

OPPOSITE *Full protection can reduce the extent and severity of injuries.*

BELOW *Mitts protect the hands, which are particularly vulnerable because of the instinctive reaction to put out your hands to break a fall.*

so that any injury caused by sliding across the road surface is much reduced.

Mitts, cycling gloves without fingers, are another injury saver. In a fall, you instinctively put out your hands to protect yourself. Gravel rash on the palms of the hands can be prevented by a good pair of mitts. Sometimes even a minor fall can result in cuts and grazes on the hands. This will make it painful to hold the handlebars for some days, can affect your training schedule, or the progress and enjoyment of a long tour.

Eyes also need protection. If your vision is even momentarily affected by something getting into the eye, it can result in a fall. Wearing normal sunglasses does provide some protection, but they aren't adequate for cycling.

One problem is that they are likely to let in the airstream and small draughts can cause the eyes to water or be irritated. Glasses designed for cycling eliminate this. Often they also have provision for different lenses to be fitted: clear lenses for riding in overcast conditions, yellow for improved visibility in the rain and dark lenses for sunny conditions.

If the expense of specialist cycling glasses is a consideration, then at least spend some time in a shop specializing in conventional sunglasses to find a pair that provides an acceptable fit to protect your eyes from the rigours of wind and dusty roads.

DEFENSIVE CYCLING

As stated in Chapter 7, when discussing the technique of riding in traffic, the first line of defence is bright, colourful clothing. This applies to most cycling situations. You are very vulnerable when sharing the road with other vehicles, and being visible is part of that defence.

Remember that you will often share the road with motorists who do not view cyclists as fellow road users, but rather as a hindrance to the progress of their journey. In a confrontation between a bicycle and a motor vehicle, the bicycle will always come off worst. Don't fight battles you cannot win.

When riding in urban traffic, don't be confrontational. If a motorist performs some silly, or even downright illegal manoeuvre that affects you, it is not worth trying to retaliate. Often the motorist will not even realize that the action taken might have endangered you.

Always signal your intentions when you anticipate having to move out of a straight line. Even when moving out a little way toward the centre of the lane to avoid a car manoeuvring into a parking space, you should indicate your intention by pointing in the direction you are planning to move, so that traffic coming up from behind can be aware of what you are about to do.

If you are riding on a road with more than one marked lane, and the lane in which you are narrows, either because of parked vehicles, or road works or any other reason, you need to ensure that a vehicle does not overtake you where there is insufficient room. To achieve this, signal first and then move out toward the centre of the lane in plenty of time to establish your position in the lane. This will make following motorists aware of your position and prevent them from trying to squeeze past you through the narrow section. As soon as the road widens, move back to the nearside, and wave a 'thank you' to cars that may have had to slow down to your pace.

Signal early, particularly if you are planning to move to another lane in order to turn off at a junction. Take particular care at traffic lights, and watch for traffic turning across the lane you are in. While they should give you the right of way, do not rely on it. Sometimes they do not see you in the clamour of city traffic and turn, thinking they are clear.

RIGHT Always signal your intentions clearly. Don't expect a motorist to anticipate your movements.

Sometimes they simply turn across, thinking that cyclists are so slow that there will be plenty of time. Either way, if you are not alert and expecting the worst, you could end up doing a practical test of your helmet.

Keep an eye on parked cars. If you see the driver is still in the car, the possibility is that he will open the door to get out of the vehicle. If the driver opens the door without checking traffic coming up behind, and you are not alert, it could result in a damaged bike and body.

If you have to commute through city streets, try to avoid routes with the heaviest traffic. Often a detour through nearby streets provides a safer, quieter environment for at least a part of the ride. Equally, if the regular route has poor road surfaces, or road works in progress, take another route, even if it takes a few minutes longer.

In traffic, defend yourself at all times; always expect the worst; and plan your ride accordingly.

Riding in traffic is not the only place where you need defensive tactics, however. In a group, there are also things you can do to protect yourself.

Always be aware of where the group is going, roughly how far and for how long they will be riding. On the ride, keep alert to what is going on around you in the group. Remember not to allow your front wheel to overlap the rear wheel of the rider in front of you.

Often in a big group, there are riders of varying abilities. Watch the riders closest to you and if there is one who rides badly, weaves about or changes speed frequently, try to find a place in the group ahead. That way, if this rider does a silly thing and causes a fall, you won't be affected.

After some distance there could be riders who are not fit enough for the pace. They may not like to admit that the pace is too fast and will exert every effort to stay in the group. Once a rider is fatigued, however, bike handling tends to deteriorate. If you see this happening, try to get the group to moderate the pace somewhat to give the rider a chance to recover.

LEFT *Hand signals are usually self-evident, but they may differ from country to country.*

ROAD MANNERS

Always ride with the flow of the traffic, keeping either to the left or the right, depending on the rule of the road in that part of the world. If another road user gives you right of way at a junction, acknowledge the civility with a wave. It gives the driver a good feeling, but more important: it indicates that you have seen the action and are turning across the driver's path.

Where there are cycle paths, it is not generally mandatory to use them in place of the normal road. However, you need to be aware of what the rules are in the area. Often, cycle paths are either designed for slow-moving utility bikes and commuting schoolchildren, or they are badly designed. Either way, many cycle paths can be more dangerous for cyclists than the road shared with motor vehicles. Where there are good cycle paths with room to safely pass slower cycling traffic, it makes sense to use them and avoid the risks inherent in riding in mixed traffic.

Stop at traffic lights. There seems to be an international fad among cyclists, believing that no matter where in the world they are, it is accepted that they do not have to stop at traffic lights. Not only is this practice dangerous and illegal, but it also strengthens the argument of those motorists who would like to see cyclists banned from the road.

Unless there are street signs specifically permitting it, do not ride on the pedestrian sidewalk. Sometimes it is tempting to take a short cut, or to avoid a road junction by riding on the sidewalk, but it does not do much for the image of cycling and cyclists. The pedestrians you upset by riding past them on a pedestrian-only sidewalk will in all probability be motorists at another time of the day.

ACCIDENTS

The legal obligations on the parties involved in an accident vary from country to country. Find out what you are required to do in the event of an accident involving another vehicle, particularly when someone is injured. However, there are also some practical steps that can and should be taken wherever you are.

Irrespective of how the accident happened, the first priority is to ascertain who, if anyone, is injured and how seriously. If you are riding in a group when the accident occurs, check if anyone in the group has medical or first aid training, then let that person take charge of the injured person.

If the accident is serious, try to get outside help. Ask if anyone in the group has a mobile phone. If not, locate a public telephone, or ask to use the

ABOVE There are many ways of making yourself more visible on a bike at night. In this instance, more is better.

phone at a residence or business nearby. Failing all that, one or two of the group should be sent to the nearest known location from where help can be summoned, while those who remain at the site can try to stop a passing motor vehicle and ask the driver to summon help.

The injured person's welfare must be your first priority. Use as many options to summon assistance as you can think of. If you are lucky, the first vehicle to stop might be able to take the injured person to a

medical centre for help, long before the rider sent ahead can get to the next town.

Once the welfare of the injured has been attended to, the cause of the accident can be investigated. If the accident did not involve anyone outside the group it should be evident whether it was caused by someone's negligence or because of some outside influence, such as a hole in the road, a broken component or a puncture.

If the accident involved another vehicle, whatever the local legal requirements might be, you should make a note of at least the registration number, make and colour of the vehicle. This really needs to be written down, but not too many cyclists carry a pen and paper, in which case the information should be committed to memory. If you have a mobile phone in the group, then the registration number can be 'saved' as if it were a phone number.

Also, try to ascertain the name and address of the driver of the other vehicle. The injured will almost certainly incur costs, which may or may not be covered by medical or other insurance. In most cases, there is likely to be some form of claim against the individual responsible for the accident.

If the local legal requirement is for the police to come out to any accident involving

injury, then remain on the scene until they arrive.

Undoubtedly, the best safety device you can carry is a mobile phone. From a simple call to one of the family to pick you up in the event of a breakdown or puncture, to summoning help in the event of an accident, it can turn potential disaster into inconvenience at the press of a button.

RIDING AT NIGHT

Never ride after dark without lights. Even during that period of diminishing light between sunset and complete darkness, a pedestrian or a cyclist becomes increasingly difficult to see from a motorcar. Even on city roadways that are well lit by streetlights you should avoid the temptation to think that you are visible just because you can see where you are going.

The minimum requirement should be a battery-powered white light facing front and a red LED (Light Emitting Diodes, requiring very little power) at the rear of the bike. Legislation differs around the world and in the UK, for instance, flashing LEDs are not legal if attached to the bike. If you want to carry a flasher in the UK, it must be attached to your clothing or rucksack. Most countries around the world insist on reflectors at the rear of the bike and that the lower part of the rear mudguard or fender be painted white. This could pose a problem if you ride on a stripped-down bike!

I avoid riding in the dark, because on some roads, in some countries, you are likely to get knocked off even if you had a neon light on your head! But if you are forced to commute or train in the dark, there are several options when it comes to selecting lighting for your bicycle. The choice probably depends on how much night riding you are likely to do.

Lights powered by replaceable batteries can become an expensive irritant to someone who commutes in the dark on a regular basis, because frequent replacement will be necessary.

Rechargeable batteries are an alternative so long as you remember to place them on charge at appropriate intervals.

Another option is a dynamo-powered lighting unit. Driven by the wheel of the bike, it provides light as long as the wheel turns. The downside is that when you stop, for instance at a controlled intersection, then you are in darkness and an approaching motorist may not see you.

Modern LEDs are terrific, though, and there are bike lights available that comprise three white LEDs requiring very little power, so that the small batteries last through the longest commute, or training session, and longer. The LEDs

also throw a very strong white light that spreads wide instead of throwing a small blob on the road that creates more shadows than it casts light. This is important if you are training along country roads without street lights. In that case it would also be helpful to use a similar lightweight LED headlight, of the type used by mountaineers and campers, that can be strapped to your forehead.

In addition to the light on your bike, the main purpose of which is to make you visible, a headlight will actually point in the direction you are looking – instead of at the sky, into roadside vegetation or the opposite side of the road – and will illuminate

what you need to see, such as the edge of the road, obstructions and potholes.

Reflective jackets or cross straps are another life-saving device to ensure that you are visible in the dark. Reflective tape on the pedals or on the back of the shoe also help because from behind they look like little lights flashing up and down, so attract attention.

Whatever other add-ons you choose to help increase your visibility, the minimum should still be a good white light at the front and a very visible red light at the rear of the bicycle.

Remember, if a motorist cannot see you, he could kill you.

LEFT *Ensure that you are visible from the side as well as from behind and the front.*

ABOVE *René Andrelet in the Tour de France prologue which is routed through the streets of Paris.*
OPPOSITE *Le Tour reaches Paris.*

ORGANIZATION OF THE SPORT

Almost as soon as the bicycle became a viable form of locomotion, people pitted themselves against each other, both on closed cycle tracks and on the road. Much of the development of the bicycle was a result of racing at the end of the 19th century, and it is still largely true as technology is continually applied to improve the bicycle in the quest for better performance.

At the same time, events aimed at being more inclusive have also come into being. In France, for instance, Audax developed, followed by its offshoot, Randonneur events. Other countries followed suit with trials and orienteering events.

However, it was not until the cycling boom that started in the late 1970s that mass participation events, in particular the Centuries so popular on the North American continent and the cyclo-sportif events in Europe, reached the

levels of popularity that they enjoy today. Major events currently draw thousands of entries and provide participants with more than simply a route to ride. The infrastructure of major events often includes closed roads, mechanical service, medical back-up, transponder timing and computerized results.

Organized events like these are a breeding ground for racing cyclists. There are many events open to riders of different categories that include a regular race over the same route as the classic races. And, of course, there are the great classic cycle races that have separate events over the route or part of the route for members of the public who are not licensed riders. L'étape du Tour, taking in a stage of the Tour de France, is a prime example, allowing riders to ride one of the stages of this great race.

During the 1990s, the UCI began to investigate their role in world cycling and decided to recognize these events. This led to the launch of the Golden Bike series, which is covered in more detail in Chapter 10.

For most of the 20th century the sport was separated into amateur and professional racing. Amateur racing was organized by amateur cycling clubs, following the rules and code laid down by the UCI, though largely ignored by that body.

During the 1960s and 1970s, there was a blurring of the two separate codes of amateurism and professionalism and soon professional promoters were running more events. It took until 1996 for all forms of cycle racing controlled by the UCI to finally become 'open' with no distinction between amateur and professional.

LICENSING

Cyclists who wish to race require a racing licence that is recognized by the UCI for domestic competition in their own country. This document is issued by the national federation, usually via the club to which they belong.

The national federation can also issue international licences permitting the holder to take part in competition in countries other than his own.

The UCI stipulates the format of the licence card (although not all countries necessarily follow this) so that the official at the start of a race sees a familiar document whether it was issued in Holland or Honduras. On international licences, a photograph of the holder is mandatory. This licence includes personal details such as date of birth and the racing category for which the rider qualifies.

The licence can be withdrawn if the competitor commits a serious breach of the rules, preventing the rider from entering other events for a period of suspension. In events where drug testing is done, it serves as positive identification of the rider being tested. The licence is an important control document that enables proper regulation of the sport.

OPPOSITE *A group of cyclists negotiates the last turn leading up to the Col de Peyresourde between Saint-Girons and Loudenvieille-le-Louron during the Tour de France.*

UNION CYCLISTE INTERNATIONALE

The international body that controls the sport is called the Union Cycliste Internationale (UCI), which was formed in 1900. This body recognizes one national federation in each affiliated country. The UCI also regulates the rules under which cycle races are run.

Each national federation recognizes local regional bodies as affiliates to which clubs are in turn affiliated.

Club officers are generally volunteers or, occasionally, part-time employees, but most often people who have made the sport a part of their lives. The regional associations to which the clubs are affiliated are also manned by volunteers, elected to their positions by members of affiliated clubs.

In most of the major cycling nations, a full-time professional staff manages the national federation, although even at that level volunteers play a major part.

The organization of these mass-participation events requires the skills of professional management groups. Some of the latter developed from clubs and grew with their event over time. Others are fully professional organizations launched specifically for the purpose of sports organization.

These organizations have people with skills in computer technology, marketing and promotional strategies, media and television, and the ability to muster large reserves of volunteers to carry out the many tasks necessary to make the event happen. They also deal with the authorities who control the public roads and facilities in the towns and villages involved in the event.

ABOVE *Riding through the feed zone between Nevers and Lyon during the Tour de France. Many mass events have acquired the same large organizational infrastructure.*

CATEGORIES

At domestic level, many national federations categorize riders by ability and provide racing restricted to one or more of those categories. Points are awarded for placings achieved in events. This tally is used to move riders from one category to another.

The UCI, however, only recognizes age categories. These are:
- Junior men (17–18 years)
- Junior women (17–18 years)
- Under 23 men (19-22 years)
- Elite men (23 years and older)
- Elite women (19 years and older)
- Masters men and women (30 and older if the rider elects this status)
- Youth (male or female riders 16 years or younger). Youth cycling is governed by national federations, who make their own rules in their area of jurisdiction.

CLUB RACING

Riders usually become involved in racing through events run by their club. These events often take the form of time trials, but also include the more popular 'bunched' races, depending on the size of the club and the abilities of the members. Handicap events often provide a basis for club events to make the competition more even.

For many club riders competing at this level, it is the first step to a serious commitment to road cycle racing as a sport. Clubs are the foundation of cycle racing.

MASS EVENTS

Major events today draw thousands of entries and provide participants with more than simply a route to ride. The infrastructure of major events often includes road closures, mechanical service, medical back-up, transponder timing and computerized results...
... and sometimes help in finding your bike.

ABOVE Félice Gimondi, after whom the Gran Fondo Félice Gimondi race was named.

OPPOSITE Cycling has become an all-inclusive sport that allows you to choose the level at which you want to participate or compete.

WOMEN

One of the first road races, the Paris–Rouen held in 1869, had a woman in its list of 37 finishers. Despite this, for many years cycle racing was not considered suitable for women. Only as late as 1958 (89 years after the Paris–Rouen) did the UCI permit the organization of the first world championship for women. The first winner of the Women's World Road Championship was Elsy Jacobs of Luxembourg.

Today there are world championships for women in all recognized age categories. There are also many multiday stage-races held around the world specifically for women.

In all forms of cycle racing women compete separately from men, but the same rules apply. Unfortunately, women's racing does not generate the same amount of publicity, sponsorship or prize money as men's racing. The incentive is less, and the competitors fewer than in men's racing.

VETERANS (MASTERS)

Until the late 1990s the UCI did not recognize a category for veterans, although most countries did so and had categories at national and local level for competitors over 35 or 40 years.

As people in the Western world generally grew healthier and had more leisure time, so racing cyclists from both the amateur and professional ranks continued to ride until later in life. This encouraged riders who had given up cycling in their youth to return to the sport. Age, however, made it difficult for more than a handful of exceptional riders to compete on equal terms with younger riders, and so more and more events were organized for veterans.

In 1970 an event was held in the small town of St Johan in the Austrian Tirol, called the Weltpokal (World Cup). Organized for racing cyclists over the age of 35 years, it quickly attracted riders from all over Europe, and soon from the far reaches of the world. It provided a week of racing for veteran riders in age categories of five-year spans, starting at 35 years.

Soon this was seen as the unofficial world championship for veterans. The winners of

each day's events were fêted with podium presentations, trophies and the familiar rainbow hoops of the World Championship jersey. For the talented riders it was a serious undertaking.

Coming as it did at a time of a worldwide cycling boom, it added impetus to the international movement toward events that were more inclusive. This made it possible for more cyclists to compete realistically, instead of bowing out of the sport because they'd lost their youthful edge or simply lacked the time or ability to make a career of racing. St Johan provided all this and it prospered.

In the 1990s the UCI recognized age categories for veterans and the Weltpokal in St Johan became the official UCI World Championship for Veterans. Today the St Johan event lasts two weeks, providing a week-long series of races for the traditional Weltpokal, followed by the official UCI-sanctioned World Masters Road Championship a week later over the same course.

MASS EVENTS ARE A BREEDING GROUND FOR RACING CYCLISTS. MANY EVENTS OPEN TO LICENSED RIDERS OF DIFFERENT CATEGORIES COVER PART OF THE SAME ROUTE AS THE CLASSIC RACES

RACING AS A CAREER

In 1996 the UCI abolished the distinction between professional and amateur. Although professionalism was effectively abolished, riders who compete in the richest races in the world earn their living by it.

This side of the sport is now controlled under the Trade Teams regulation of the UCI.

There are three levels of Trade Team or *groupe sportif*.

GS1 teams (TTI) are the top teams in terms of money and talent. These are the teams whose names are household words; who compete before a worldwide TV audience in the major events on the international calendar. These are the riders who contest the three great Tours: the Vuelta in Spain, the Giro in Italy and the most famous cycle race of all – the Tour de France.

GS2 (TTII) is the second division of the sport. The better ones often blend in with the GS1 teams in some of the races, but more often become the stars of lesser events. These teams are often the starting point for talented young riders making a first move into the harsh world of cycle racing at the highest competitive level. The GS2 teams also have riders

---

∴ SERIOUS ROAD RACING

Road cycle racing requires considerable dedication and single-mindedness from those who compete at anything more than club level. It is a highly complex, well-organized and very structured sport.

As with most sports today, success can lead to riches, and those who are attracted to the sport of racing a bicycle often have that possibility in mind.

Road cycle racing is an attractive and colourful sport which, thanks to international television coverage, has become a worldwide sport understood by many who have never raced, or considered racing themselves.

Professional racing has driven bicycle design ever since 1869 when the 22-year-old English doctor, James Moore, won two of the first cycle races ever held. Today it still drives design as the specialist bicycle manufacturers supply mass-produced replicas of Trade Team bicycles so that competitors in mass-participation events can enjoy the same level of technological development.

When you wheel your modern lightweight cycle out of the garage, you have a lot to thank the professional racer for.

OPPOSITE *Serious riding requires the kind of single-minded determination that will have a cyclist completing a race with a fractured collarbone. Here Tyler Hamilton climbs up to the Col Bagarguy between Pau and Bayonne during the Tour de France.*

reaching the end of their careers and who have dropped out of GS1 teams, but have a wealth of experience to pass on to the younger riders coming into the sport. GS2 is also the stepping stone for teams and sponsors wanting to compete at the highest level, and who seek promotion to GS1.

The third level is GS3 (TTIII). These teams have the lowest budgets. The riders are generally not as talented as those in the two higher categories, although there will be some talented young riders biding their time to break into the bigger teams.

These Trade Teams race worldwide in events listed on the UCI calendar, which includes single and multi-day stage races. The UCI maintains a ranking list of teams and riders, with annual promotion and relegation of teams between the three levels. Riders and teams score points for placings, the number of points depending on the event. For example, a place gained in a stage of the Tour de France would score many more points than a win overall in a minor event in a country outside Europe. Individual riders use their annual score of UCI points to negotiate a place on a better team when the season ends.

RIGHT *Many of the mass-participation events today offer the same organizational infrastructure as the classic tours, such as road closures and medical and mechanical back-up services.*

MASS-PARTICIPATION EVENTS

A SAMPLE OF SOME OF THE GREAT EVENTS

The sport of cycling offers many choices in the way you can spend your time riding. Organized rides offer the camaraderie of like-minded people, safety and technical back-up. These can be close to home, or you can experience the excitement of riding in an international event. Many of these offer a greater challenge than local events and require long-term planning and training. Around the world there are hundreds of events that offer something out of the ordinary — here we can merely scratch the surface.

RIGHT *Participants in the Gran Fondo Félice Gimondi race.*

OPPOSITE *The mass start to a mass participation event can be a challenge in itself.*

EVENTS DEVELOP INTO
GROUPS OF RIDERS WHO
WANT TO DO THE DISTANCE
IN THE SHORTEST POSSIBLE
TIME AND THOSE WHO JUST
WANT TO ENOY THE RIDE
AND THE SCENERY

1 GRAN FONDO FELICE GIMONDI

Date: *Early May*

City: *Bergamo, Italy*

Long route: *165.3km (102.7 miles)*

Height difference: *2260m (7415ft)*

Medium route: *134.5km (83.6 miles)*

Height difference: *1671m (5483ft)*

Short route: *95.7km (59.5 miles)*

Height difference: *1194m (3918ft)*

⁖ Information

G.M. SPORT
Via Da Campione 24/B,
Bergamo, Italy
Telephone +39 035 211721
Fax +39 035 4227971
info@felicegimondi.it
www.felicegimondi.it
www.felicegimondi.com

This is the most important of the many Italian cyclo-tourist, or Gran Fondo events, and was the UCI's choice for the Golden Bike Series. Named after one of Italy's great champions, the event offers three different distances, with the longest of the three offering a major challenge to any cyclist. It includes over 2200m (7200ft) of climbing, including the Colle del Gallo (the Rooster Hill) at 763m (2503ft), Selvino at 962m (3156ft) and Berbenno at 661m (723ft), all used in the professional Giro di Lombardia stage race.

2 LE MONDIAL/ CYCLOTOUR DES CANTONS

Date: *July*

City: *Québec, Canada*

Categories: *MW, Enterprise and Club – all 125km (78 miles)*

⁖ Information

Le Mondial du Vélo.com 3
ch. de Gaspé, C.P. 39 Bromont
Québec, J2L 1A9 Canada
Telephone +1 450-534-2453
Fax +1 450-534-1832
info@mondialduvelo.com
www.mondialduvelo.com

ABOVE *The start of the Gran Fondo Félice Gimondi.*

3 CAPE ARGUS PICK 'N PAY CYCLE TOUR

Date: Second Sunday in March
City: Cape Town, South Africa
Route: 109km (68 miles)
Height difference: 250m (820ft)

> **Information**

Cape Town Cycle Tour Trust
Events office
PO Box 777, Rondebosch
Cape Town 7701, South Africa
info@cycletour.co.za
www.cycletour.co.za

The Cape Argus Pick 'n Pay Cycle Tour is the world's largest timed cycle race. It has grown from a first event with 525 cyclists in 1978 to a field now limited to 35,000 cyclists for safety reasons.

OPPOSITE Entries of 35,000 require staggered starts and seeding.

4 L'ARDÉCHOISE

Date: June
Venue: St Felicien, Ardèche region, France.

> **Information**

l'Ardéchoise – BP 4
07410 St Felicien
www.ardechoise.com

L'Ardéchoise is the biggest of the mass-participation cycling events in France. Held in the Ardèche region of southern France, the first event was on 20 June 1992. The 1296 entrants for that first event were faced with a torrent of rain and freezing cold; on the heights of the Gerbier de Jonc pass it was snowing! The following year the participants faced scorching heat.

L'ARDÉCHOISE

Circuit	Distance km (miles)	Cols (Mountain passes)	Climb metres (feet)	Timed Cyclo-sportif	Untimed Cyclo-tourist
Le Doux	66 (41)	2	1081 (3547)	1 day	–
Les Boutières	120 (75)	5	2122 (6962)	1 day	2 days
La Volcanique	171 (106)	8	3042 (9981)	1 day	1 or 2 days
L'Ardéchoise	216 (134)	10	4117 (13,508)	1 day	1 or 2 days
Les Sucs	223 (139)	14	4100 (13,452)	1 day	1 or 2 days
L'Ardéchoise Velo Marathon	268 (167)	16	5175 (16,979)	1 day	1 or 2 days
La Loire	284 (176)	16	5529 (18,141)	–	2 days
Les Hautes Terres	336 (209)	21	6419 (21,061)	–	2 days
L'Ardèche	312 (194)	16	6184 (20,290)	–	2 days
Le Tanargue	364 (226)	22	7072 (23,203)	–	2 days

L'Ardéchoise grew from 3268 participants in 1994 to 6857 in 1996 when Patric Bruet, nicknamed The Prince of Cyclosportives, set a time of 06h09. A year later the Russian Andreï Kivilev covered the route in 05h49. That year saw the entry reach 9818 participants.

In 1998 the event was enlarged to include new routes. By 2003 the event exceeded 15,000 entrants and was the biggest timed cycling event in Europe.

The organizers of L'Ardéchoise offer a choice of circuits to make the event accessible to riders of all fitness levels.

ABOVE *One of the scenic towns on the route of L'Ardéchoise.*

5 LA MARMOTTE
Date: *July*
City: *Bourg d'Oisans, France (closest major centre is Grenoble)*
Distance: *174km (108 miles)*
Height difference: *5000m (16,405ft)*

⫶ Information
*The organizers Top Club and Sport Communication
BP 61 – 38242 Meylan Cedex – France
Telephone
+33 (0)4 76 00 01 54
Fax +33 (0)4 76 03 16 67
info@sportcommunication.com*

The start in Bourg d'Oisans is at the foot of Alpe d'Huez. The route through Isère, Savoie and into the Alps involves climbing over famous passes such as the Croix de Fer (2068m; 6785ft), Le Telegraphe (1570m; 5151ft), Le Galibier (2642m; 8668ft), Le Lautaret (2057m; 6749ft), and the famous 21 hairpins of the Alpe d'Huez (1495m; 4905ft) to the finish at the ski resort. There are refreshment stations at Valloire (97km; 60 miles), and Bourg d'Oisans (161km; 100 miles).

La Marmotte was one of the first cyclo-sportive events that developed from randonneur rides. La Marmotte is probably one of the most difficult because its 174km (108-mile) route crosses four of the giant passes sometimes featured in the Tour de France to finish at the top of the most famous. It attracts some 5500 entrants, mostly from Holland. Despite the July date, the weather on the high passes is often very wet and cold, adding to the challenge of the event.

Le Bourg d'Oisans is the capital of the Oisans region, in that part of France known as the Dauphine. Situated in a valley between the Alpe d'Huez and Col du Galibier, the town is an ideal centre for any form of cyclo-touring.

6 NEW YORK CITY CENTURY BIKE TOUR

Date: September
City: New York, USA
Routes:
1. 24km (15 miles)
2. 56km (35 miles)
3. 88km (55 miles)
4. 120km (75 miles)
5. 160km (100 miles)

⋮⟩ Information

Transportation Alternatives
115 West 30th Street
12th Floor
New York, NY 10001
Telephone +212 629 8080
Fax +212 629 8334
info@transalt.org
www.transalt.org/calendar/century

With more than 4000 entrants the NYC Century Bike Tour is one of the biggest centuries in the United States, although not the largest cycling event

in the country. That honour goes to Bike New York, a 68km (42-mile) parade of cyclists held in May each year, which attracts more than 30,000 cyclists.

The NYC Century Bike Tour follows a route of bike lanes, greenways, parks and low-traffic streets through the city of New York. There are a few short unpaved sections and (on some of the five available routes) a few blocks of cobble-stoned road-surface. There are five refreshment stations.

All five rides start and finish at Central Park's Harlem Meer, and then link NYC's spectacular bridges and parks. The more experienced and competitive riders can choose between the 121km (75-mile) or 161km (100-mile) routes.

The 121km (75-mile) route follows the perimeter of Brooklyn and Queens, while the 161km (100-mile) route follows the same course, but includes a loop around the great Bronx greenways.

The NYC Century Bike Tour attracts a wide spectrum of riders. From beginners to experienced cyclists, from family groups to racers, the Century is intended to be a fun day of riding, whether participants are socializing and exploring or facing up to a competitive challenge.

These major mass-participation events are but the tip of the iceberg. There are thousands more around the world. And for those who don't want someone else to organize their recreational time, there is the open road. The freedom that only the bicycle can give. It is yours. The cost? The impetus to start, the rest is pleasure.

ABOVE Brooklyn Bridge at sunrise – one of the bridges on the route of the New York City Bike Tour, which attracts more than 30,000 cyclists each year.

LINKS AND CONTACTS

BICYCLE MANUFACTURERS

www.bassobikes.com
Basso Italian cycles

www.bgcycles.com
Bruce Gordon specialist touring cycles

www.cannondale.com
Cannondale bicycles and accessories

www.colnago.com
Colnago bicycles

www.giant-bicycles.com
Giant bicycles

www.kleinbikes.com
Klein bicycles

www.lemondbikes.com
LeMond bicycles

www.raleighbikes.com
Raleigh bicycles

www.robertscycles.com
Roberts cycle frame builders

CENTURIES

www.active.com/century_challenge
One-stop access to Century and Double Century events.

www.transalt.org/calendar/century
New York City Century

CLUBS AND FEDERATIONS

www.adfc.de
Allgemeiner Deutscher Fahrrad-Club (Germany)

www.atlanticcanadacycling.com
Atlantic Canada Cycling

www.audax.uk.net
UK Audax club

www.bfa.asn.au
Bicycle Federation of Australia

www.britishcycling.org.uk
Cycling Federation of Great Britain

www.canadian-cycling.com
Canadian Cycling Association

www.can.org.nz
Cycling Advocates' Network (New Zealand)

www.ctc.org.uk
Cyclists Touring Club (UK)

www.ecf.com
European Cyclists' Federation

www.cyclingireland.org
Cycling Ireland

www.federciclismo.it
Federazione Ciclistica Italiana

www.ffc.fr
Fédération Française de Cyclisme

www.fietsersbond.nl
The Dutch Cyclists Association

www.pedalpower.org.za
Recreational cycling in South Africa

www.rfec.com
Real Federación Española de Ciclismo

www.sa-cycling.com
A site on South African cycling

www.uci.ch
International Cycling Union (UCI)

www.usacycling.org
USA Cycling

ACCESSORIES

www.avocet.com
Tyres, saddles and computers

www.bellbikehelmets.com
Cycle helmets

www.bikeprousa.com
Cycle bags and packs

www.brookssaddles.com
Leather saddles

www.camelbak.com
Hydration systems

www.campagnolo.com
Campagnolo group-sets

www.carradice.co.uk
Cycle panniers and packs

www.cateye.com
Cat Eye cycle computers

www.ciclosportusa.com
Cyclometers, heart-rate monitors

www.cinelli.it
Components and frames

www.giro.com
Cycle helmets

www.headlandbike.com
Racks, mudguards, multi-tools

www.irc-tire.com
Tyres

www.lookcycle.com
Pedals, frames and forks

www.mavic.com
Wheels, rims, components

www.michelin.com
Tyres

www.niterider.com
Lighting

www.oakley.com
Eyewear

www.ortlieb.de
Panniers and cycle bags

www.panaracer.com
Tyres

www.panniers.com
Touring panniers

www.philwood.com
Sealed bearing hubs

www.scicon.it
Touring panniers

www.selleitalia.com
Saddles

www.serratus.ca
Touring panniers

www.shimano-europe.
   com/cycling
Smimano group-sets and
derailleurs

www.sidiusa.com
Sidi cycling shoes

www.specialized.com
Touring panniers

www.speedplay.com
Clipless pedals

www.thethirdhand.com
Specialized cycle tools

www.timesportusa.com
Clipless pedals; frame-sets

www.zefal.com
Pumps, bottles and accessories

EVENTS

www.ardechoise.com
The biggest cyclo-tourist event
in France

www.bikenewyork.org
Largest mass-participation
event in the United States

www.ledauphine.
   com/challenge
French event for cyclosportifs
and cyclotouristes

www.letour.fr
Tour de France

www.radmarathon.at
Cycle marathons in Austria

PUBLICATIONS

www.adv-cycling.org
Adventure Cycling
magazine, USA

www.bicyclingmagazine.com
Bicycling Magazine, USA

www.bicyclingaustralia.com
Bicycling Australia

www.bike.com
Online cycling magazine, USA

www.cyclesportmag.com
Cycle Sport Magazine,
UK and USA

www.cyclingnews.com
Cycling News, Australia

www.cyclingplus.co.uk
Cycling magazine, UK

www.procycling.com
ProCycling magazine, USA

www.velonews.com
Cycling magazine, USA

www.velovision.co.uk
Specialist cycling magazine
covering recumbents

TOURING

www.bigfoot.com/~rctc
Cycle touring in Russia

www.cyclenewzealand.com
Pre-arranged cycle tours

www.kenkifer.com
Tips for tourists

www.mayq.com
European touring

www.northsea-cycle.com
North Sea cycle route

http://nypca.org/canaltour/
Erie Canal cycling tour

www.telemark-tours.no
Non-competitive tours
in Norway

OTHER

www.bhsi.org
Bicycle Helmet Safety Institute

www.spokeswomen.
pwp.blueyonder.co.uk
Women's cycling

:: GLOSSARY

ALLEN KEY: Hexagonal bar bent at 90°, used to tighten hex bolts

ANSI Z90.4: Bicycle helmet safety standard of the American National Standards Institute

ATTACK: To accelerate or break away from other cyclists during a competition

AUDAX: Special touring events with checkpoints

BALL BEARING: Hard round spheres, usually of steel, set in series between two bearing races with cups and cones, or in a sealed cartridge

BASE TRAINING: A preparatory period usually consisting of long periods of riding; also referred to as base miles, or base work

BIKE BOOM: Historic period of cycling popularity, the first in the 1890s and the second beginning around 1970

BLOCK (1): To slow or disrupt the progress of another cyclist, to disrupt the chase of a breakaway

BLOCK (2): A cassette or multi-speed freewheel

BONK: To run out of energy; to exhaust stored glycogen

BOTTOM BRACKET: The axle to which the driving cranks and pedals are attached

BRAKE LEVER: The operating lever for a brake system, fitted to the handlebar

BRAKE SHOE (OR BRAKE PAD): Part of the brakes that comes in contact with the wheel rim to stop the bike

BREAK OR BREAKAWAY: One or more cyclists leading, separated from the main group

BROOM WAGON: a support vehicle on a ride or race that follows the last rider or group on the course, to pick up riders who have abandoned the race

BUNCH: Main group of cyclists; also field, pack, or peloton

CADENCE: Rate of pedalling measured in revolutions per minute

CALLIPER BRAKE: Brakes that operate through a pair of callipers exerting leverage to both sides of the rim

CAMBER: The slope from the crown to the edge of a road, path or track, designed to aid drainage. Off-camber bends or curves in the road slope away from the apex and force a vehicle toward the outside of a turn

CAMPY OR CAMPAG: Shortened name for Campagnolo, an Italian manufacturer of bicycle racing components

CARBO LOADING: Dietary method of increasing energy supply for specific athletic events

CENTURY: A 100-mile (161km) ride; a metric century is 100km (62 miles)

CHAIN-GANG: a group of cyclists who get together for training sessions

CHAINSET: The cranks and large sprockets attached to the bottom bracket and through which the cyclist applies power to propel the cycle

CLINCHER OR WIRE-ON: Tyre with separate tube that fits onto the rim by a beaded belt

CLIPLESS: A step-on pedal that has a built-in shoe-cleat retaining system

CLUB RIDE: Group rides organized by cycling clubs for regular, dedicated touring or training

CYCLE PATH: Road or trail dedicated for cycling, often shared with pedestrians and joggers, also called bikeway, bike path, or cycleway

CYCLE-TOURING: Touring by bicycle; usually including camping with camping gear and luggage

CYCLO-TOURIST: Cyclists who compete in mass-participation events. These events are often based on the classic races, or cover one of its stages

CREDIT CARD TOURING: Touring with little or no luggage, and relying on the purchase of food and shelter at the end of each day

DANCE (ON PEDALS): To ride out of the saddle, usually on a hill climb, with a quick cadence

DERAILLEUR: The mechanism that moves (de-rails) the chain from one sprocket to another to alter the gear ratios

DIAMOND FRAME: The most common bike frame design. It has a diamond shape

DRAFTING: Riding behind another cyclist or vehicle to gain aerodynamic advantage

DROPS: Lower part of the handlebars, usually below the brake levers

DROPOUTS: The slot in the rear fork stays into which the rear wheel axle fits and is fixed by a wheel nut or quick release mechanism

ECHELON: A pace-line of cyclists drafting each other, usually grouped in two staggered lines, taking turns to move forward into the wind, while the others are sheltered

FORK: Two-bladed component that attaches the front wheel to the bike, providing steering. The stem and handlebars connect to the top of the fork

FRAME: Main structural part of the bike to which all components are attached

FUNNY BIKE: Name given to aerodynamic bikes made in the 1980s

GRADIENT: Steepness of an incline, measured in percentage (100m rise in 1km = 10% gradient)

GRANNY GEAR: Very low gear, used for steep hills and carrying loads

HANDLEBAR: Control component of the bike – where you place your hands

HANDLEBAR STEM: Component that connects the handlebars to the forks

HEADWIND: Wind resistance from the front that limits the speed of cycling

HEART RATE: Heart beats per minute

HONK: Out-of-the-saddle acceleration by standing on pedals, pulling on handlebars, moving the bike side to side. Style also used on a steep climb

HOODS: The portion of the brake lever attached to the handlebars that can be used as a hand grip

HUB: The centre of the wheel. It rotates on bearings around the axle. Spokes attach the hub to the rim of the wheel

ISO (INTERNATIONAL STANDARDS ORGANIZATION): Organization that sets world standards – also for bicycle materials, component sizes and threadings

JUMP: A quick acceleration that may develop into a breakaway or sprint, usually out of saddle, standing on the pedals

MOTORPACE: Riding in the draft of a motor vehicle

PACELINE: Chain-like formation of cyclists sharing the pace by taking turns at the front of the group to break the wind, then pulling aside and soft pedalling while dropping to the sheltered rear position for rest (*see drafting, echelon*)

PAVÉ: Cobblestoned road surface

PELOTON OR PACK: The whole or main group of cyclists

PRESTA VALVE: Air valve commonly used on high-pressure tubes and tubular tyres

PRIME: (pronounced preem) A mid-race sprint for a prize, points, or time bonuses

QR (QUICK RELEASE): A lever and cam system that permits the wheels to be fitted or removed from the frame without tools. A similar system is built into most brake callipers permitting them to open wider to allow easy removal of the wheel

RANDONNEUR: (also called randonnée or rando) Special touring event with checkpoints. Similar to Audax

RIM TAPE OR STRIP: A strip of fabric, plastic or rubber used to line the rim, which covers the spoke nipples to prevent the tube from being punctured by the end of one of the spokes

RIM: Part of the wheel into which the tyre fits

ROAD RASH: Skin abrasions resulting from a fall on the road surface

SAG WAGON: Motor vehicle following cyclists in tours or races that carry equipment, clothes, food, medical supplies, and tired or injured cyclists (*see also broom wagon*)

SEW-UP: (also tubular tyre) Tyre with the casing sewn around the inner tube

SIDEWALL: Side of the tyre

SLIPSTREAM: Wind shelter provided by leading cyclist or group

SNAKEBITE: One or two tiny punctures in a tube, usually caused by under-inflated tyres and/or hitting a hard object such as a big stone or the curb

SOFT PEDAL: Half coasting, half pedalling, turning the pedals with minimal force to save energy

SPIN: Pedalling at a rapid cadence

SPOKE: Part of the wheel. A system of metal wires that attach the rim to the hub and give the wheel shape and strength

SPOKE NIPPLE: Accepts the threaded end of the spoke and is used during truing to adjust the wheel

TREAD: The rubber on the outer edge of a tyre, often with a pattern moulded into it for better traction

TRUING: Process of making a wheel round by adjusting tension in the spokes through the spoke nipples

TUBE: Inner tube to hold air for the tyre and give it shape. Part of the wheel. Fits between the tyre and the rim

TUCK: Aerodynamic position used for descending

TYRE: Part of the wheel. An inflatable rubber and fabric casing into which is fitted a tube that contains air under pressure, providing a lightweight contact with the road surface

TYRE LEVER: Tool usually sold in pairs, made out of metal or plastic, which is used to lever the tyre from the rim

UCI: (Union Cycliste Internationale) The world controlling body for cycling

VALVE: Usually a part of the tube, enabling the tyre to be inflated

VALVE STEM: Pin in the centre of the valve with a threaded retaining nut, which can be depressed, after unscrewing the nut, to open the valve and release air from the tube

≋ INDEX

PHOTOGRAPHIC CREDITS AND ACKNOWLEDGEMENTS

DEDICATION
To Carol who puts up with me and who even took up the sport of cycling for me.

AUTHOR'S ACKNOWLEDGEMENTS
I would like to thank: The staff of New Holland Publishing for this opportunity, and particularly Alfred and Anna for their enthusiastic support; Gillian and her team for making my words look attractive on the printed page and Gerhard and his bikeriders for letting us take the photographs.

PHOTOGRAPHIC CREDITS

ABBREVIATIONS USED

PICTURE POTITIONS t=top, l=left, r=right, b=bottom, c=centre.

AGENCIES AND PHOTOGRAPHERS: ARD = www.ardechoise.com; BAL/AC = Bibliothèque des Arts Decoratifs, Paris, France/Bridgeman Art Library/Archivs Charmet; BAL/RP = Private Collection/Bridgeman Art Library/Roger Perrin; CoC = Company of Cyclists; CND = Cannondale; CP/CB = COMetaPRess/Carlo BRena; GI = Gallo Images/gettyimages.com; JP = Jason Patient; NHIL/NA = New Holland Image Library/Nicholas Aldridge; NHIL/WH = NHIL/Warren Heath; NHIL/DN = NHIL/Danie Nel; ME = Mary Evans Picture Library; PA = Photo Access; PB = Photo Brenton; SF/BS = Stockfile/Bob Smith; SF/SB = Stockfile/Steven Behr; SF/SR = Stockfile/Seb Rogers; SIL/JM = Struik Image Library/Jacques Marais; TA/DB = Transportation Alternatives/ David Begelfer; TA/GC = Transportation Alternatives/ Gregory Cross; TA/JK = Transportation Alternatives/Joyce Kiley; TA/KZ = Transportation Alternatives/Ken Zirkel; TLP = Touchlinephoto.com

f/cover	GI	15	CoC	79	TLP	104	TLP	135	TLP
b/cover	TLP	16	SF/BS	81	TLP	105b	JP	136	TLP
2–3	TLP	18	JP	82	SIL/JM	106–107	TLP	138	TLP
4–5	SF/SR	21	PB	83	TLP	109	TLP	139	TLP
6	TLP	23t	SIL/JM	86–87	TLP	110–111	TLP	140	CP/CB
8	GI	23b	JP	88	SIL/JM	113	TLP	141	GI
9	BAL/RP	24b	JP	90–91	TLP	116–117	TLP	142–143	TLP
10	ME	26	PA	92	SIL/JM	120b	SF/BS	144–145	TLP
11t	CoC	27t/r	CND	93	NHIL/DN	121	GI	146	CP/CB
11c	ME	28b	TLP	94–95	NHIL/NA	122	JP	147	TLP
11b	ME	32	NHIL/NA	96–99	NHIL/WH	123	SF/BS	148	TLP
12t	ME	50	TLP	100t	NHIL/DN	130–131	JP	149	CP/CB
12b	ME	58–59	TLP	101b	NHIL/DN	132	SF/SB	150–151	TLP
13	BAL/AC	62	SF/SB	102	TLP	133	SF/SB	152	ARD
14	GI	64	SIL/JM	103t	TLP	134	TLP	153	TA/GC